THE OFFICE GUIDE

SECOND EDITION

Levsit

LINDA MALLINSON

Prentice
Hall

Editor-in-Chief: Stephen Helba
Executive Editor: Elizabeth Sugg
Editorial Assistant: Anita Rhodes
Production Editor: Brian Hyland
**Director of Production
  and Manufacturing:** Bruce Johnson
Maniging Editor—Production: Mary Carnis
Manufacturing Buyer: Cathleen Petersen
Design Director: Cheryl Asherman
Cover Design: Kevin Kall

PearsonEducation LTD.
PearsonEducation Australia PTY, Limited
PearsonEducation Singapore, Pte. Ltd
PearsonEducation North Asia Ltd
PearsonEducation Canada, Ltd
PearsonEducación de Mexico, S.A. de C.V.
PearsonEducation -- Japan
PearsonEducation Malaysia, Pte. Ltd
PearsonEducation, Upper Saddle River, New Jersey

10 9 8 7 6 5 4
ISBN 0-13-094524-2

CONTENTS

iii

GP 4   SEMICOLON

GP 5   COLON

GP 6   QUOTATION MARKS

GP 7   HYPHEN

GP 8   APOSTROPHE

vi

PREFACE

The primary purpose of this office guide is to help transcription operators and others produce correctly written and formatted documents. The guide presents the basic rules of grammar, punctuation, word usage, and document formatting. Résumé formats, information about international and domestic mail, and filing rules are also included. Spelling of troublesome city names and places are given, and special features of word processing software are noted in relation to document formatting.

The Office Guide is designed to be used as a supplemental text to *Transcription Skills for Business*. It can be used, however, as a stand-alone reference. Proofreading, grammar, punctuation, and formatting exercises covering the rules and information in *The Office Guide* are integrated in the 16 lessons of *Transcription Skills for Business*. The wide use of word processing software has produced some controversy concerning traditional document formatting; and new trends have resulted in changes to some punctuation, spacing, and usage rules. These new technology-driven changes have been noted in this second edition of *The Office Guide*.

GENERAL REFERENCE

GR 1 CONFUSING WORDS

Many words sound or look alike but have different meanings. Other words are just plain troublesome. Below are some of the most common words that fall into these two categories.

Accede: Sanction, comply with, consent or agree to. (The staff had no choice but to <u>accede</u> to the contract.)
Exceed: To go beyond. (She will <u>exceed</u> her budget allocation by $250.)

Accent: To emphasize; characteristics of a manner of speech. (The <u>accent</u> is on the first syllable. He has an <u>accent</u>.)
Ascent: Rise. (The song's <u>ascent</u> to the number one position in a week was remarkable.)
Assent: Concur, agree. (Did he <u>assent</u> to chair the next committee?)

Accept: To acquire, take, or receive. (We will <u>accept</u> credit cards.)
Except: To omit or exclude. (Everyone was invited <u>except</u> him.)

Access: Entrance, admittance. (We didn't have <u>access</u> to the computer lab.)
Excess: Extra. (The <u>excess</u> paper will be recycled.)

Ad: Advertisement. (The <u>ad</u> will appear in Tuesday's paper.)
Add: To increase or join. (We will <u>add</u> two class sections in May.)

Adapt: To adjust or change. (We will have to <u>adapt</u> the program to meet our needs.)
Adept: Skilled or proficient. (Mary is very <u>adept</u> at keyboarding.)
Adopt: To select. (The board will <u>adopt</u> the suggested bylaw changes.)

2

Addition: Something added. (The <u>addition</u> to the house increased its market value.)

Edition: One version of a printed work. (The fifth <u>edition</u> of the text included information about certification.)

Adherence: Attachment, constancy, abiding. (Her <u>adherence</u> to the rules helped her win.)

Adherents: Followers, fans, disciples. (The <u>adherents</u> of Dr. Loe's philosophy will meet in June.)

Adverse: Unfavorable; harmful effect; hostile. (The drug was produced under <u>adverse</u> conditions; and because it wasn't tested enough, patients using it had an <u>adverse</u> reaction.)

Averse: Opposed, reluctant to agree. (The teachers were <u>averse</u> to the contract proposal.)

Advice: (noun) Information or recommendation. (Ann Landers gives good <u>advice</u>.)

Advise: (verb) To recommend or counsel. (The doctor will <u>advise</u> him to quit smoking.)

Affect: (verb) Impact, involve; to alter; influence or change. (The tuition waiver will <u>affect</u> all students.)

Effect: (noun–consequence, result) or (verb–bring about). (The <u>effect</u> of the policy changes will impact only new employees. The new laws will <u>effect</u> a change in many policies.)

Aid: To help or give assistance. (She will <u>aid</u> him in creating the new logo.)

Aide: An assistant. (She was his <u>aide</u> in the art department.)

Air: Atmosphere. (The <u>air</u> was heavy with pollution.)

Heir: Beneficiary. (He was the only <u>heir</u> to the family's fortune.)

Err: To make a mistake. (To <u>err</u> is human.)

Aisle: Walkway, passage path. (The <u>aisle</u> is blocked by shopping carts.)

Isle: Island. (The <u>Isle</u> of Nexus is a beautiful place to visit.)

I'll: Contraction for I will. (<u>I'll</u> lower the sails on the boat when we reach the channel.)

Alley: A passageway, path. (The <u>alley</u> between West and Central Streets was crowded.)

Ally: Someone who agrees with your position, to unite for a specific purpose. (She was his <u>ally</u> when the departments were merged.)

Allot: Allocate, distribute, or set aside a certain amount. (It was decided to allot one-fifth of the budget for technology training.)

A lot: Many; much. Note: "Alot" is NOT a word. (She had <u>a lot</u> of supporters who contributed <u>a lot</u> of money to her campaign.)

Almost: Nearly. (Janie <u>almost</u> fell asleep during his boring presentation.)

All most: Everyone very much; clue—the word "most" can be left out of the sentence and it would still make sense. (We are <u>all most</u> pleased with the new office furniture.)

Allowed: Permitted. (Alice was <u>allowed</u> to go to the party.)

Aloud: Audible, verbally, out loud. (She read the names <u>aloud</u>.)

Allusion: An indirect reference, hint, suggestion. (If you carefully analyze the historical literature, you will find many <u>allusions</u> to unethical political ploys.)

Illusion: Hallucination, false impression. (Because he drove an expensive car and lived in an exclusive neighborhood, he gave the <u>illusion</u> that he was wealthy; but he had declared bankruptcy.

Elusion: Avoidance. (His <u>elusion</u> of commitment was evident in his refusal to marry Elaine.)

Already: Previously; earlier. (The students had <u>already</u> toured the department on a field trip.)

All ready: Completely ready; prepared. (The story was <u>all ready</u> for press when the news broke.)

Altar: Tabernacle; religious platform or table. (The <u>altar</u> was decorated with flowers.)

Alter: Change. (She had to <u>alter</u> her plans to go to the party from work.)

Alternate: Substitute; take turns. (His <u>alternate</u> at the meeting is Ruth. They will <u>alternate</u> attending meetings.)

Alternative: One of several choices or options. (The only <u>alternative</u> he had was to resign.)

Altogether: Entirely. (The cost of the book was <u>altogether</u> too expensive!)

All together: As a group. (They left the party <u>all together</u>.)

Always: At all times; constantly, continuously. (She is <u>always</u> late.)

All ways: Every choice, option, or method. (The team explored <u>all ways</u> to make training convenient and decided that a Saturday morning workshop was best.)

Analyst: Software system consultant; investigator; analyzer. (The computer <u>analyst</u> charged $100 an hour.)

Annalist: Historian, clerk. (At 105 years of age, Peter's grandfather is the town's <u>annalist</u>.)

Annual: Yearly. (The <u>annual</u> Christmas party was canceled.)

Annul: Cancel. (She can <u>annul</u> her marriage.)

Ante: Prefix meaning before; cost, price; to pay up. (During the antebellum period, the ante for poker games was high; however, after the Civil War few poker players could afford an ante of any kind.)

Anti: Prefix meaning against, opposed to. (The antipoverty campaign spread quickly to other neighborhoods.)

Any one: Any item or person in a group. *Hint—spell as two words when followed by the preposition of.* (Any one of your teachers can recommend you.)

Anyone: Anybody; one person. (Did anyone see where I put my keys?)

Anyway: In any case; regardless; anyhow. (She will not be at the meeting anyway, so you can preside.)

Any way: By any method. (We will raise the money any way we can.)

Appraise: Evaluate; to set a value. (The auctioneer will appraise the merchandise.)

Apprise: To inform. (The new chairman will apprise us of our options.)

Arraign: To call a defendant to court, charge, to accuse of wrong. (Sally was arraigned on five counts of perjury.)

Arrange: To put in order. (She will arrange the files so that the most recent correspondence is in the front.)

Assistance: Help, support. (She offered her assistance to the new employee.)

Assistants: Individuals who help. (Her assistants all received top salaries.)

Attendance: Number present. (The attendance at the theme park was down from the previous month.)

Attendants: Escorts; an employee who assists customers. (The parking lot attendants received overtime for working last Thursday.)

6

Awhile: Hint—use one word when used as an adverb for a short time. (We will wait <u>awhile</u> before leaving for the party.)

A while: Hint-use two words when used as a noun for a short period of time. (Once in <u>a while</u> we will miss the bus. It was <u>a while</u> back that I saw him.)

Bare: Empty; naked. (The cupboard was <u>bare</u>.)

Bear: Animal. (The <u>bear</u> was shot.)
Keep in mind, harbor. (Please don't <u>bear</u> a grudge.)
Support. (The roof couldn't <u>bear</u> the weight.)

Bases: Plural of base and basis. (There were many <u>bases</u> to cover before leaving.)

Basis: Foundation. (The <u>basis</u> for the new curriculum is cooperative learning.)

Baited: Teased; lured. (He <u>baited</u> her into taking the new job with promises of fast promotions and better benefits.)

Bated: Restrained, deduct. (She waited with <u>bated</u> breath to see if she made the team.)

Beat: To hit; win; tired. (She easily <u>beat</u> him in the race because he was so <u>beat</u> by the third lap he couldn't keep up.)

Beet: Vegetable. (She sliced the <u>beet</u> and added it to the stew.)

Beside: Next to; by the side. (She stood <u>beside</u> him on stage when he repeated the loyalty oath.)

Besides: In addition to. (<u>Besides</u> the pay increase, the staff received more vacation time.)

Biannual: Occurring twice a year. (The next <u>biannual</u> sale is in May.)

Biennial: Occurring once in two years. (The conference is a <u>biennial</u> event.)

Bizarre: Strange. (His bizarre behavior frightened everyone.)

Bazaar: A place where goods are sold. (The church bazaar is a revenue-making event.)

Billed: Advertised; charged. (He was billed as the fastest typist. The attorney billed the client for five hours of work at $80 per hour.)

Build: Construct; make. (Mr. Smith can build a desk in two days.)

Board: Timber. (The boards used for the deck were treated to prevent bug damage.)

Bored: Dull; pierced. (The students were bored watching him bore the wood to make holes in it.)

Boarder: A person who pays for meals and lodging. (The boarder stayed two days.)

Border: Edge. (She added a border around her address on her flyer.)

Born: Natural; brought into life. (He was a born leader.)

Borne: Carried, endured. (The air borne pollutants caused serious health problems.)

Brake: To stop; a device for slowing or stopping. (The brakes on her car needed $400 worth of repairs.)

Break: An opportunity; to divide; fracture, destroy. (Her break into management came when her boss retired, which caused a break in her friendship with her colleagues.)

Bread: Food. (She toasted six slices of bread.)

Bred: Upbringing; past tense of breed. (She was bred to respect her elders.)

Breath: Respiration. (Her breath could be seen in the cold air.)

Breathe: Inhale and exhale. (Her punctured lung made it hard to breathe.)

8

Breadth: Magnitude; scope; width. (The breadth of the door made it possible to put the piano in the study, and this is where she practiced a breadth of music ranging from classical to country.)

Broach: To bring up; propose. (She was afraid to broach the subject of his transfer.)

Brooch: A jewel. (The brooch she wore to the ball was very expensive.)

Burrow: Hole for an animal. (The rabbit hid in his burrow.)

Borough: A town. (As a child he lived in the borough that borders this city.)

Calendar: Record of time. (The calendar for meetings is now kept on the computer.)

Calender: To press between rollers; machine used in finishing paper. (The calender needed to be repaired so the production of the book had to be postponed.)

Colander: Strainer. (Mary received a colander for a shower gift so it will be easier for her to cook spaghetti now.)

Cannot: Unable. Format that is usually used. (We cannot honor your request because we are out of that item.)

Can not: Must not. (We can not miss the boat.)

Canvas: Coarse cloth used for painting. (The painting was very fragile because the canvas was old.)

Canvass: To solicit; campaign. (The students will canvass the area to gain support for the new student union.)

Capital: Main; sum of money; punishable by death; seat of government. (The capital needed for the new student union will be obtained from Mr. Smith who is the capital supporter of this venture.)

Capitol: Edifice; building where legislative bodies meet. (The capitol needs a new roof and major repairs.)

9

Center

Carat/karat: A unit of weight (200 milligrams) used to measure precious stones. (The chain was 24 <u>carat</u> gold.)

Caret: Mark (Λ) used to show where something is to be inserted. (It took a long time to make the revisions because the proofreader used 25 <u>carets</u> to indicate changes.)

Carrot: Vegetable. (The horses enjoyed the <u>carrots</u> the child fed them.)

Cash: Ready money. (The <u>cash</u> was stolen yesterday.)

Cache: A storage place, something stored in a special hiding place; Internet garbage in a hidden recycle bin. (You should empty the Internet <u>cache</u> frequently to keep your computer running efficiently. His <u>cache</u> of gold coins was stolen.)

Cease: Terminate, stop. (Her mother told her to <u>cease</u> seeing her new boyfriend.)

Seize. To capture, take. (She will <u>seize</u> the opportunity to go back to school.)

Ceiling: Top of a room. (The <u>ceiling</u> was leaking.)

Sealing: Closing. (<u>Sealing</u> the tomb was a major undertaking.)

Census: Population statistics. (The <u>census</u> is taken every ten years).

Senses: Reasoning ability. (Her <u>senses</u> were impaired after the accident.)

Cereal: Breakfast food. (Mary put sugar on her <u>cereal</u>.)

Serial: In a series, continuing. (The <u>serial</u> novels were best sellers.)

Choose: To select. (Because of her inheritance, Fran could <u>choose</u> whether or not to send her daughter to private or public school.)

Chose: Selected; past tense of choose. (Fran <u>chose</u> to send her son to public school.)

Chord: Musical tones. (The students needed to learn several chords.)

Cord: Rope; an electrical cable with plugs at each end. (The student tripped over the electrical cord.)

Chronic: Long duration, constant. (She had chronic bronchitis.)

Chronicle: Events in order of time; history. (Mary will establish a chronicle of the school and publish it.)

Cite: Quote, call. (As part of their test, students had to cite examples of each substance.)

Sight: Vision. (His sight was hampered when his glasses broke.)

Site: Place. (We didn't have a site large enough to hold the conference.)

Click: A slight, sharp noise; pressing on a computer mouse; to fit together, "hit of." (When you click on the computer mouse, it frequently makes a click. Mary and Todd were so different that they did not click.)

Clique: An exclusive group. (She was depressed because she was not able to join the clique of girls who were popular on campus.)

Cliché: Trite phrase. (He used several clichés in his campaign speech.)

Clothes: Garments. (Her clothes were not appropriate for a job interview.)

Cloths: Fabrics. (The cloths came from all over the world.)

Close: To shut. (Close the door when you leave.)
Near. (The building was close to the gas station.)
Intimate. (They had a close relationship.)

Coarse: Rough. (The sandpaper was very coarse.)

Course: A direction; part of a meal; part of a curriculum. (How many elective courses we can take will depend upon the course of action the student government takes on the proposed changes.)

Corpse: Dead body. (The corpse was found in the old mill.)

11

Collision: Accident, colliding, clash. (The collision between the two trucks happened at noon.)

Collusion: A scheme to defraud. (Tyler was not part of the collusion to deceive the bank's clients.)

Command: An order; to direct, lead. (The command to stop made the thief slow down. He will command the troops.)

Commend: To praise. (John, I commend you on your recent promotion.)

Commence: Begin. (The ad campaign will commence on June 10.)

Comments: Remarks. (Her comments caused several people to leave.)

Complement: Supplement, round out. (The belt she is wearing complements her outfit.)

Compliment: Praise. (She had a hard time accepting compliments from her friends.)

Comptroller: Financial official who audits government accounts and certifies expenditures. (The comptroller was responsible for finding discrepancies in the city's financial records.)

Controller: Chief accounting officer of a business or educational institution; one who has the power to control. (The controller found problems with the reimbursement procedures used in the university's Education Department and recommended several changes.)

Confidant: A friend. (John has been one of Tom's closest confidants.)

Confident: Sure. (He was confident that Sally could do the job.)

Confidently: Certainly. (She presented her proposal to the board confidently.)

Confidentially: Privately. (Confidentially, between you and me, Sue did not win the nomination.)

Conscience: Psyche, knowing right and wrong. (Marty's <u>conscience</u> would not allow him to cheat on the test.)

Conscious: Aware, cognizant. (He was <u>conscious</u> after the accident.)

Conservation: Preservation. (Recycling is one example of our effort toward <u>conservation</u> of our national resources.)

Conversation: A discussion. (During the course of the <u>conversation</u>, we learned he moved.)

Council: A committee, advisory board. (The City <u>Council</u> will decide if the proposal should be placed on the ballot.)

Consul: A foreign representative. (The German <u>consul</u> was very helpful.)

Counsel: An attorney; give advice. (His counselor will <u>counsel</u> him about career choices.)

Core: Heart, central part. (The <u>core</u> of the design will center around the new addition.)

Corps: Military troops, a group sharing a common interest. (The teachers involved with the Peace <u>Corps</u> still keep in touch with each other.)

Correspondence: Letters. (One of the items that drew the most bidding was Elvis Presley's <u>correspondence</u>, which was auctioned for $30,000.)

Correspondents: People who communicate through writing; journalists. (Years ago when they were young, they were war-time <u>correspondents</u>.)

Cue: A hint. (Sally took her <u>cue</u> from John when delivering her lines.)

Queue: A line. (The documents were <u>queued</u> to the printer, and Joan joined the <u>queue</u> waiting for her letter to print.)

Dairy: A source of milk products. (Women need calcium from <u>dairy</u> products.)

Diary: Daily journal. (At thirteen, Mary faithfully wrote in her <u>diary</u>.)

Decent: Proper or ethical. (The <u>decent</u> thing to do is to return the wallet.)

Descent: Falling, going down. (The <u>descent</u> from the cliff was difficult.)

Dissent: Conflict, disagreement (The new manager made it clear he would not tolerate any <u>dissent</u> among his staff concerning the new guidelines.)

Defer: Delay, postpone. (Until we have more members present, we will <u>defer</u> making the decision.)

Differ: Disagree; unlike. (The two candidates <u>differ</u> on their view of the issue of state regulation.)

Deference: Respect, honor. (In <u>deference</u> to his aunt's wishes, he did not leave.)

Difference: Dissimilar, variance. (The <u>difference</u> between their ages made their marriage fun.)

Deposition: Formal written statement. (The attorney took his <u>deposition</u> on Tuesday morning.)

Disposition: Temperament, nature. (Jonathan's calm <u>disposition</u> made him an ideal manager.)

Desert (dez'ərt): Dry, barren land. (The <u>desert</u> was extremely hot and dry.)

Desert (di-zûrt'): Abandon; leave. (He promised not to <u>desert</u> her.)

Dessert (di-zûrt'): Treat; sweet food; *"Just Dessert"* reward. (She saved her <u>dessert</u> for last. He received his <u>just dessert</u> when he received the promotion.)

Detract: Take away. (His late arrival <u>detracted</u> from the speaker's presentation.)

Distract: To divert attention. (She tried to <u>distract</u> Jim's attention from his studying.)

14

Device: A gadget, tool. (The device he used to pry open the lock looked like an altered screwdriver.)

Devise: To plan, to bequeath, to transmit. (The committee members worked hard to devise a more dynamic advertisement campaign. Mary received real property from a devise in her aunt's will.)

Discreet: Tactful, diplomatic. (Tom was discreet in his negotiations for the supervisor's job because he did not want to upset the current manager.)

Discrete: Distinct, separate units, not mathematically continuous. (The discrete problems assigned for homework involved working with several infinite numbers.)

Dew: Moisture. (The dew on the grass made her shoes wet.)

Do: Perform. (She will do her chores later.)

Due: Unpaid; owed. (She asked for the balance that was due on their account.)

Disburse: To make a payment, to pay out, expend from a fund. (The treasurer will disburse the reimbursement funds at the end of the month.)

Disperse: To scatter. (The groups of protesting students should disperse once the police arrive.)

Done: Finished. (The report had to be done by noon on Friday.)

Dun: Repeated demand for payment. (We will dun him for the entire amount over the next six months.)

Dual: Two. (The dual exhaust pipes on his car were expensive to replace.)

Duel: A fight. (They were both injured in the duel.)

Elicit: Extract, to draw forth, to evoke a response. (She tried to elicit the information from John about who had been selected to replace him on the board, but he did not divulge the person's name.)

Illicit: Unlawful. (He didn't know it was illicit to sell alcoholic beverages on Sunday. He was arrested for illicit behavior.)

Eligible: Qualified. (He was eligible for the reward.)

Illegible: Unreadable. (His handwriting was illegible.)

Elusive: Baffling; hard to catch or pin down. (His strange, elusive behavior made it difficult to determine whether he was telling the truth.)

Illusive: Deceptive, misleading. (Martha was put on probation at school because Sandra gave the dean illusive information about Tuesday's meeting.)

Emerge: Come out, to become known. (The baby chick began to emerge from the shell.)

Immerge: To plunge into or to immerse oneself in something. (He immerged into silence.)

Emigrate: To leave a country. (Each year thousands of people emigrate from their homes in other countries to come to the United States.)

Immigrate: To come into a country and establish permanent residency. (When did she immigrate to the United States, and when did she become a citizen?)

Eminent: Well-known, prominent. (He was an eminent journalist.)

Immanent: Inherent, residing within. (His immanent desire to be a good person leads him to perform acts of kindness.)

Imminent: Impending, near, threatening. (The storm put everyone in imminent danger.)

Ensure: Make certain. (His hard studying will <u>ensure</u> good grades.)

Insure: Guarantee, protect against loss. (He needs to <u>insure</u> his car.)

Assure: Convince. (He tried to <u>assure</u> his daughter that she would always be welcome in his house.)

Envelop: Wrap. (The mist will <u>envelop</u> the valley in a haze.)

Envelope: Mailer for a letter. (The <u>envelope</u> got wet and the writing smeared.)

Everyday: Routine, common, frequent. (His <u>everyday</u> routine included going to the school.)

Every day: Daily, each day. (His mother told him to wash his clothes <u>every day</u>.)

Everyone: Everybody. (<u>Everyone</u> in the Accounting Department did not read the Email message; therefore, no one from that department came to the meeting.)

Every one: Each person or thing in a group. *Hint: two words when followed by "of."* (<u>Every one</u> of the students had books with <u>every one</u> of the pages incorrectly numbered.

Expand: To increase. (His territory will <u>expand</u> when he becomes the regional supervisor.)

Expend: To spend, use up. (He will <u>expend</u> his cash reserves quickly if he is not careful.)

Fair: Impartial; rainless; favorable; average; mediocre; usual; exhibit/event. (There was a <u>fair</u> (average) turnout at the <u>fair</u> (exhibit with entertainment) because the weather was <u>fair</u> (not stormy) and the judges were <u>fair</u> (impartial) in their scoring of the competitors.)

Fare: Travel; to get along in terms of progress; transportation fee; food. (The <u>fare</u> for the voyage included breakfast <u>fare</u>. He didn't <u>fare</u> too well on the journey and was seasick.)

Farther: Distance: (The farther you go from home, the harder it is to return.)

Further: In addition; more; greater degree. (If you further your studies, you will get a promotion.)

Flair: Aptitude, style. (Tom had a flair for writing poetry.)

Flare: To become angry; a light, a signal, to burn. (His temper began to flare when he saw the flare in the distance because he knew the children had disobeyed him and gotten into the toolbox.)

Forgo: To relinquish; to let pass. (Jean will forgo the opportunity to become supervisor because her husband will be transferred.)

Forego: To go before; precede. (The treasurer's report will forego the new business discussion.)

Formally: Officially. (He was dressed formally for the occasion.)

Formerly: Before. (Her name was formerly Anderson.)

Forward: Ahead. (Sally was looking forward to retirement.)

Foreword: Preface of a book. (The foreword in the book gave an overview of the author's life.)

Guarantee: Assurance, agreement. (Sara guarantees that the new lipstick will moisturize the user's lips and has agreed to refund unhappy customer's money if it doesn't.)

Guaranty: Something given as security, pledge, guarantee; promise to answer for another's debt. (Julie gave Tim her watch as a guaranty that she would pay him what she owed him.)

Hall: Public building; entrance, corridor. (The hall was crowded with people making it difficult to keep the hall leading to the kitchen clear.)

Haul: To drag or move; the quantity transported; load. (He will haul the haul he won at the fair to his house.)

18

Hear: Audio input; listen. (Sally didn't <u>hear</u> the siren because her radio was so loud.)

Here: This place. (Be sure you are <u>here</u> at 5 p.m.)

Heard: Past tense of heard; listened to; was informed. (Jonathan <u>heard</u> about the contest from his friend.)

Herd: Assemble; a group of animals; a pack. (Mr. Romely tried to <u>herd</u> the frightened <u>herd</u> of cattle into the barn during the storm.)

Higher: Above, beyond. (The <u>higher</u> you go in the organization, the more responsibility you will have.)

Hire: Employ. (We will <u>hire</u> John to help set up the lab.)

Hoard: Save; keep to oneself; hidden supply. (He <u>hoards</u> his comic books and shares them with no one. His brother found his <u>hoard</u> of comic books where he had stashed them in the attic.)

Horde: Crowd. (The <u>horde</u> of shoppers made it difficult to get to the sale items.)

Holy: Sacred, blessed. (The temple is considered to be a <u>holy</u> building.)

Holey: Full of holes. (Do not wear that <u>holey</u> shirt to the play.)

Wholly: Completely. (Sara gave herself <u>wholly</u> to becoming an artist.)

Human: Person; related to mankind. (Because the computer isn't <u>human</u>, it doesn't understand <u>human</u> nature and only gives error messages.)

Humane: Kindly, compassionate. (Mary worked for the <u>Humane</u> Society and was touched by the <u>humane</u> treatment given to the animals.)

Implied: Suggested. (Mary's comments <u>implied</u> that the new manager was strict.)

Inferred: Assumed. (From Mary's remarks, the new employee <u>inferred</u> that she should get to work on time.)

Incidence: Occurrence. (There is an unusually high incidence of radiation readings.)

Incidents: Events, happenings. (Numerous incidents of poor health habits were noted.)

Incinerate: To burn. (If you don't have a paper shredder, I suggest that you incinerate the manuscript to protect the author's identity.)

Insinuate: To imply. (Did she insinuate that he got the promotion?)

Incite: Provoke (verb). (The new policy requiring people to work more hours each month incited the workers who threatened to strike.)

Insight: Understanding; intuition. (Her insight into the conflict was very valuable since no one else was familiar with the culture of the region.)

Indict: Formally accuse or charge. (Tony believes the jury will indict Robert for the crime.)

Indite: Write; compose, dictate. (The new office manager will indite a new procedures manual.)

Indifferent: Apathetic, uncaring. (She was indifferent to his romantic interest.)

In different: In other; more than one. (She will speak to several students in different rooms.)

In regard to: Never use *in regards to*; leave off the *s*. Correct form is *in regard to*. (In regard to your request for a charity donation, contact our customer service representative.)

Instants: Short periods of time. (It was several instants before he could move.)

Instance: Example. (We will receive less revenue, for instance, from clothing sales.)

Its: Possessive of it. (She ripped <u>its</u> pretty wrapping in order to open the box.)

It's: Contraction of it is. (<u>It's</u> time for us to leave.)

Later: After a time. (We'll meet for lunch <u>later</u>.)

Latter: Refers to something previously stated; second of two things; following. (I have the October and November issues of the Microsoft Office magazine; the <u>latter</u> has an article on merging.)

Lay: To place. (Do not <u>lay</u> the book on top of the stove.)

Lie: Noun meaning falsehood; verb meaning to recline. (He told a <u>lie</u> so that he would not be punished and miss the dance. She had to <u>lie</u> down because she felt faint.)

Lye: A strong alkaline solution. (The <u>lye</u> caused Shawn to break out in hives.)

Legislator: Lawmaker. (He was sued for libel because of the unkind and false remarks he made about the <u>legislator</u>.)

Legislature: A group of lawmakers. (The <u>legislature</u> was comprised of a lot of young, first-time members.)

Lead: When pronounced like *led* means a heavy metal. When pronounced like *leed* means to guide or influence; go first. (The <u>lead</u> used in the paint many years ago caused health problems. He will <u>lead</u> the group on the hike.)

Led: Past tense of *to lead* meaning influenced, guided. (His research <u>led</u> to the discovery of penicillin. He <u>led</u> the expedition into the rain forest.)

Leased: Rented. (We <u>leased</u> the car for four years.)

Least: Smallest, minimal. (She had the <u>least</u> amount of work to do. At <u>least</u> he could have said goodbye before he left.)

Lessen: To make smaller (verb). (She could do little to lessen his grief over his wife's death.)

Lesson: Assigned exercise; education. (Jean's lesson was to research the history of computers. He learned his lesson when he burned his hand on the stove.)

Liable: Responsible. (He was liable for paying his daughter's medical bills.)

Libel: Published defamatory remarks, slander. (He was sued for libel because his story was derogatory and untrue.)

Loose: Free, unrestrained. (The dog got loose from the yard.)

Lose: Fail to win, misplace an item. (She thinks she will lose the election if she loses her lucky charm.)

Loss: Damage; something lost. (She suffered a financial loss.)

Maybe: Perhaps. (Maybe we can go to the park after lunch.)

May be: Verb form, might. (Sally may be on vacation for three weeks.)

Moral: Virtuous; honest; good; lesson. (Mrs. Thompson was a very moral person. The moral of the story is to always tell the truth.)

Morale: Spirit, confidence. (The morale of the staff was low until the new supervisor arrived.)

Morning: Early part of the day. (She had a hard time getting up in the morning because she stayed up so late.)

Mourning: Expressing grief. (She was in mourning for a long time after her mother's death.)

Past: Finished or ended; go by; previously in time. (We went past his house last week, which is where he has been living for the past eight years.)

Passed: Approved; met a grade or criteria. Past tense of pass. (We passed his house last night and left a note telling him he passed his test.)

Patience: Composure enduring over time. (She lost her patience with the screaming child.)

Patients: Sick people. (The patients had to wait an hour for the doctor.)

Peace: Quiet harmony, security. (The signing of the new treaty should help bring peace to the two countries.)

Piece: A portion or part of something. (He received five pieces of silver.)

Peak: Top, climax. (He reached the peak of his career when he was promoted to vice president.)

Peek: Glance, fast look. (She took a peek at the salary sheet while her supervisor was on the phone.)

Pique: Excite, irritate, offend. (The flyer piqued his interest in taking the course, but he was piqued when he was put on a waiting list for six months.)

Perfect: (Pur/fíkt) Adjective. Faultless; (Pêr/fekt) Verb: to improve; strive for perfection. (She was the perfect hostess. She spent hours trying to perfect her golf swing before the tournament.)

Prefect: An official. (Nancy Toland was the prefect appointed to the state advisory council.)

Persecute: Oppress, annoy, harass. (Even today people are persecuted because of their religion.)

Prosecute: Press charges, sue. (We will prosecute the trespassers.)

Peer: Colleague, someone of the same age or rank; look steadily. (Her peers gave her a surprise birthday party. Hoping to catch site of him, they peered into the distance.)
Pier: Dock. (The boat was tied to the pier.)

Personal: Private. (She had personal reasons for not going.)
Personnel: Staff. (All personnel employed by the store received a 10 percent discount.)

Perspective: Viewpoint; put into proportion. (His perspective put the cost of the project in perspective in relation to the amount of work needed.)
Prospective: Anticipated. (The prospective change in plans made everyone nervous.)

Peruse: Read. (She will peruse the proposal.
Pursue: Chase. (She will pursue her dream of going to medical school.)

Physical: Relating to the body. (He had to pass a physical before he was allowed to take physical education.)
Fiscal: Pertaining to finances. (The fiscal year will end in July so all outstanding bills must be paid by then.)

Plain: Undecorated; prairie; evident or obvious. (Remains of the plain log cabins built on the plain made it plain to see that the pioneers were good carpenters.)
Plane: Airplane; level; a carpenter's tool. (The plane circled several times before its plane stabilized enough for the passengers to remove their seatbelts. The carpenter could not find the plane, and couldn't complete the project.)

Precede: Go before; pave the way. (A raffle will precede the auction.)
Proceed: Continue. (Mr. Jones will proceed when the guests are seated.)

Precedence: Priority. (Mr. Davis's ruling will take precedence over Ms. Johnson's.)

Precedents: Established rules; something done or said that may justify the same outcome in similar situations. (The new chairperson will follow the precedents that are already in place. Prior rulings established precedents in dividing the land.

Principal: Leader; main; money drawing interest. (The principal of the school was late and didn't have time to introduce the principal members of the fund raising committee who pay the principal on the loan.)

Principle: Rule. (Several principles for success were given at the meeting.)

Presence: Being present. (His presence was requested at the dinner.)

Presents: Gifts. (They received many presents from relatives at Christmas.)

Prophecy: A prediction. (His prophecy that the town would be annexed to the city upset many people.)

Prophesy: To predict, foretell. (He would prophesy about the end of the world for hours.)

Quiet: Not noisy. (The students were quiet.)

Quite: Entirely; totally. (She was quite busy.)

Respectably: Fit to be seen. (He was dressed respectably for the occasion.)

Respectfully: In a courteous manner. (People should treat each other respectfully.)

Respectively: In the order given. (The first, second, and third place awards will go to Sara Jones, Amy Smith, and Tom Adams, respectively.)

Right: Correct; privilege. (Wendy was right in defending her rights.)

Rite: Ceremony. (His rite of passage into manhood was celebrated.)

Write: Inscribe. (They promised to write to each other)

Role: Part. (The <u>role</u> she played in the merger was significant.)

Roll: List; revolve. (Mrs. Anderson couldn't find her class <u>roll</u>. He will <u>roll</u> down the hill.)

Root: Underground plant growth, foundation. (Completely bury the <u>root</u> on the roses when you plant them. Money is the <u>root</u> of all evil.)

Route: To send or direct; course, travel plan; itinerary. (Please <u>route</u> the message that shows the best <u>route</u> to take to get to Millie's party.)

Scene: Setting; incident. (The last <u>scene</u> in the play was shortened because the two actors caused a <u>scene</u> with their fighting.)

Seen: Past participle of see. (She was last <u>seen</u> at Betty's house.)

Soar: To fly. (The bird will <u>soar</u> above the marshes once its wing is mended.)

Sore: Painful; irritated. (She had a <u>sore</u> throat.)

Someday: On any day. (<u>Someday</u> the school will have new computers and current software.)

Some day: Related to a specific time frame. Follows a preposition. (The meeting is scheduled for <u>some day</u> next week.)

Someone: A person. (We couldn't find the keys because <u>someone</u> misplaced them.)

Some one: One of a number of things. Hint: Two words when followed by *of*. <u>Some one</u> of the books has the author's signature.)

Sometime: Eventually, at some unscheduled time, in the future. Hint—use as one word when sometime follows a preposition. (The computers will be shipped sometime next week. At sometime in the future we will get new computers and software.)

Some time: A phrase in which *some* modifies *time* and designates an *amount of time*. (It was some time before she was promoted.)

Sometimes: Occasionally, now and then. (Sometimes we have to work overtime.)

Stationary: Fixed. (The building was stationary and couldn't be moved.)

Stationery: Writing paper. (Her stationery was scented with roses.)

Statue: A carved or molded figure. (The statue of Lincoln was placed in the park.)

Stature: Height, physique; status gained by achievement. (His diminutive stature did not make a difference in his highly regarded stature in the community.)

Statute: A law. (School principals take a course in educational law so that they are familiar with the statutes that require legal action.)

Suite: Office space; connecting rooms in a hotel; group of things in a unit. (The company rented a suite for her at a nearby hotel while she worked on the project.)

Sweet: Sugary, agreeable. (The candy was too sweet and made her sick.)

Than: Conjunction. Used to show a comparison or a difference. (She would rather work the first shift than the second. Few people type faster than she does.)

Then: At that time, used to indicate when. (We will go to the party first and then to Tom's house.)

Their: Belonging to them. (Their house burned.)

There: In a particular place. (We'll be there at 3 p.m.)

They're: Contraction for *they are*. (They're ahead of schedule.)

Thorough: Complete. (He had a thorough physical.)

Through: Finished; succeeding by perseverance; by means of. (She got through the rigors of school and got a job through a temporary agency.)

Threw: Hurled. (Jonathan threw the ball as far as he could.)

To: Preposition toward. (He went to law school.)

Too: Also. (She went to law school too.)

Two: The number after one. (She had two jobs.)

Trail: Path. (Susan followed the trail back to the car.)

Trial: Hardship; examination of civil or criminal cause; experiment. (It was a trial for him when he was on trial for falsifying the results of trial drug tests.)

Undo: To open; to reverse, to render ineffective. (The undo feature on the computer will take you back to the previous step. She will undo all her hard work to get the promotion if she continues to arrive late.)

Undue: Improper, excessive. (There was undue pressure on her to make the honor role since her mother was the teacher.)

Vain: Useless, fruitless; superficial. (I hope her efforts to get on the Dean's List were not in vain. Margo is very vain.)

Vane: Piece of metal used to indicate wind direction. (The weather vane showed the wind coming from the east.)

Vein: Channel, blood vessel; stratum of ore or coal; vascular tissue in a leaf. (The nurse had difficulty locating a vein to take her blood.)

Vice: Position; moral depravity or corruption. (Millie was vice president of the citizen's vice squad.)

Vise: Clamp; grip. (The vise wasn't tight enough to clamp the pieces together.)

Waiver: Relinquish claim to. (She signed a <u>waiver</u> of her right to the inheritance.)

Waver: To hesitate. (John didn't <u>waver</u> in his decision to change jobs.)

Weak: Not strong. (She was <u>weak</u> after her illness.)

Week: Seven consecutive days. (It was a <u>week</u> before she was able to come back to work.)

Weather: Atmospheric conditions. (The <u>weather</u> will be sunny.)

Whether: If. (Please see <u>whether</u> Nancy can join us for dinner.)

Were: Past plural of *is*, form of *to be*. (We <u>were</u> present when he received the award, but we wished we <u>were</u> on stage.)

Where: Someplace. (Did Tom say <u>where</u> he was Friday?)

Whose: Possessive of *who*. (<u>Whose</u> pants were left on the porch?)

Who's: Contraction of *who is*. (<u>Who's</u> going to the party?)

Your: Pronoun. (It was <u>your</u> responsibility to clean the house.)

You're: Contraction of *you are*. (<u>You're</u> ten minutes late.)

GR 2 OTHER TROUBLESOME WORDS

A and **An**. Use *a* before all consonant sounds including *h*, long *u*, and *o* with the sound of *w*.

a wonderful day   a unit   a one-way ticket

Use *an* before all vowel sounds except for long *u* and before words beginning with a silent *h*.

an open-door policy   an hour   an angel

Among: Preposition used with more than two people or things. (The supervisor must choose from <u>among</u> the five final candidates for the job.)

Between: Preposition used with only two people or things. (The dessert was split <u>between</u> the two women.)

Anxious and **Eager**: Anxious means worried. Eager means enthusiastic. Example:

Because she hadn't studied, Sally was <u>anxious</u> about passing her test.

Tim was <u>eager </u>to get his first paycheck.

Angry and **Mad**: Angry means enraged or irate. Mad means insane. Example:

Mr. Anderson was <u>angry</u> because Sara received the promotion instead of him.
The stray dog contracted rabies and went <u>mad</u>.

Bad and **Badly**: Bad is an adjective and should be used with *feel, look, sound, taste, smell, appear,* and *become.* Use badly when an adverb is needed. Example:

I feel <u>bad</u> that I was not able to go.
She was <u>badly</u> injured in the accident.

Bring and **Take**: *Bring* means to deliver to where the speaker is, and *take* means to carry away from where the speaker is. Example:

She should <u>bring</u> all her reports about the incident to me, and I will <u>take</u> them to the review committee.

Can: Have the ability. (She <u>can</u> go to the concert since she isn't working that night.)

May: Be permitted. (<u>May</u> I have the night off so that I can go to the concert?)

Despite: Means in spite of. (Despite his willingness to learn, he was unable to master all the math formulas and failed the test.)

Export: Send goods out. (The price of the goods was high due to the export tax.)

Import: Receive goods. (There is a limit on the amount of tomatoes we can import from Mexico.)

Good and **Well**: **Good** is an adjective meaning attractive, admirable, wholesome; to be in good spirits. (She was in good spirits because of her good grades. Her good looks made others envious.)

Well is an adjective used in relation to health and as an adverb meaning in a satisfactory or favorable manner. (Sally doesn't feel well. Mr. Tucker's project was well received. She performed well on the test.)

In depth: Two words. Means thoroughly or extensively. (She studied the report in depth.)

In spite: Two words. With hatred or contempt. (She tore the pages out of his book in spite.)

In spite of: Means in disregard or defiance of; despite, notwithstanding. (In spite of the snowstorm, she arrived at work on time.)

Intrastate: Occurring in one state—intra means within. (The intrastate tax should help finance new roads.)

Interstate: Occurring between states. Hint: inter means between. (The new interstate highway between Florida and Georgia should save motorists time in driving from one state to the other.)

Learn and **Teach**: **Learn** means to acquire knowledge. **Teach** means to give or impart knowledge. Example:

Mary can teach Sally how to do the math problems, but Sally must do the homework to learn the procedures.

31

Leave and **Let**: **Leave** and its forms (left, leaving) mean to move away or to depart; quit; remain in the same state without interruption; to let stay; or to let remain behind. **Let** and its forms (letting) mean "to permit or allow." Example:

Before Dr. Thompson could <u>leave</u>, he had to <u>let</u> his office staff know where to reach him. Sally <u>let</u> us use her car to go shopping. Do not <u>leave</u> the drink on the desk because it will <u>leave</u> watermarks. <u>Leave</u> the new student alone so she can study.

Less and **Fewer**: **Less** refers to an amount and should be used with singular nouns. **Fewer** refers to a number or something that can be counted and should be used with plural nouns. Example:

<u>Less</u> activity takes place on the Internet between 1 a.m. and 6 a.m. The company received <u>fewer</u> customer complaints after the staff went to training.

Raise and **Rise**: **Raise** and its forms (raised and raising) mean to lift or increase. **Rise** and its forms (rose, risen, and rising) mean to ascend or to get up. A clue to correct usage is that "raise" requires an object and "rise" does not. Example:

The heat in the building <u>has been rising</u> over a period of time, and we now have to <u>raise</u> the shareholders' awareness of the situation so that we can <u>raise</u> enough money for new air conditioning equipment.

Set and **Sit**: **Set** and its forms (set and setting) mean to put something somewhere. It also means to determine or fix. **Sit** and its forms (sat and sitting) mean to take a seat. Example:

Mary will <u>set</u> the date for her transfer to coincide with the selling of her house.

She <u>set</u> the boxes on the shelves.
April will <u>sit</u> next to Tom at the meeting.

Shall and **Will**: Use shall with I and we. (I <u>shall</u> be home by 10 p.m., and he <u>will</u> be home by 11 p.m.)

Which, That and **Who**: **Which** and **that** are used with places, animals, or things. Which should be used with nonessential clauses, and that should be used with essential clauses. **Who** is used to refer to people. Examples:

<u>Who</u> is going to the store? (Person)
The new computers, <u>which</u> arrived last week, did not include keyboards. (Nonessential clause)
<u>That</u> computer is going on sale next week. (Essential)

GR 3 FOREIGN WORDS

As business transactions become more global, the need to understand frequently used foreign words becomes increasingly important. These foreign expressions have become mainstreamed into the English language.

ad hoc	for a specific purpose
ad valorem	according to the value
a la carte	items in a meal priced separately
a la mode	served with ice cream
aplomb	sureness; sophisticated style
apropos	fitting
au jus	served in natural juices, a gravy
avant-garde	new or experimental
bona fide	real, genuine; in good faith
carpe diem	enjoy now (seize the day)
carte blanche	unconditional power, full authority
cause celebre	a noteworthy event
circa (c. or ca.)	approximately
confer (cf.)	compare
connoisseur	expert; critical judge
coup d'état	a sudden overthrow of a government
debut	first public appearance
du jour	of the day as in soup du jour
encore	again; additional performance
esprit de corps	group spirit
et al (et al.)	and others (note: "al" is always followed by a period)
et cetera (etc.)	and so forth
exempli gratia (e.g.)	for example
ex post facto	after the fact; done after
facade	front of a building; outward appearance
fait accompli	an accomplished fact
faux pas	a mistake; blunder

finesse	to handle with skillful maneuvering
hors d'oeuvres	appetizers
ibidem (ibid.)	in the same place
id est (i.e.)	that is
idem	the same
infra	below
in toto	completely, whole
ipso facto	by the fact itself
joie de vivre	joy of living
laissez faire	no interference; let alone
loco citato (loc.cit.)	in the place cited
modus operandi (M.O.)	the way in which something is done
motif	pattern or decorating theme
noblesse oblige	obligation of power
nolle prosequi (nol. pros.)	to be unwilling to prosecute
non sequitur (non seq.)	it does not follow
nota bene (N.B.)	note well
opere citato (op cit.)	in the work cited
passé	out of date or style
per annum	for each year
per capita	for each person
per diem	for each day
per se	by itself
pro tempore (pro tem.)	for the time being; temporarily
proximo (prox.)	in the next month
Q.E.D.	which was to be demonstrated
quid pro quo	something given or received for something else
quod vide (q.v.)	which see
RSVP	please reply
re (in re)	in the matter of; concerning
rendezvous	a meeting place; secret meeting

sans	without
savoir faire	self-assurance
status quo	existing state of affairs; current status
supra	above
tête-á-tête	private conversation
verbatim	exactly–word for word
videlicet (viz.)	namely
vice versa	the other way around
vis-à-vis	face to face, opposite

Foreign Address Terms

Calle, Laan, Road, Rue, Rua, Straat, Strasse, and **Via** are used to designate "street" in addresses. **Chaussée** is the equivalent to the word "route."

Bâtiment, Edificio, House, Immeuble, Palazzo, Tour, and **Torre** are common local names for buildings outside of the United States.

GR 4 PROOFREADERS' MARKS

EXAMPLE OF MARK	MEANING	CORRECTION
‖ Align text so it is ‖even.	align vertically	Align text so it is even.
⌓ This should begin a paragraph *bold*	begin paragraph	This should begin a paragraph
The term quid pro quo was new to her.	bold	The term **quid pro quo** was new to her.
born in the usa	capitalize	born in the USA
⌐ City Names ⌐	center	City Names
take o͡ut extra spaces	close up	take out extra spaces
take it out	delete	take out

Mark	Meaning	Result
DS This should be double spaced.	double space	This should be double spaced.
no ¶ He had a flat tire and didn't have a spare.	No paragraph	He had a flat tire and didn't have a spare.
The rangers, ~~teachers,~~ *stet...* and assistants will give presentations.	Ignore correction (retain text crossed out).	The rangers, teachers, and assistants will give presentations.
We̸should go̸and Sally should go too	insert space, insert comma, insert period.	We should go, and Sally should go too.
Bring your blanket and beach ball. ⓐ suntan lotion, sun glasses	insert new text	Bring your blanket, suntan lotion, sun glasses , and beach ball.
The Novel was written by Michener in 1991. *ital*	Italics	The *Novel* was written by Michener in 1991.
Her Good deed	lower case	Her good deed
This word should not be below the other text.	move up	This word should not be below the other text.
This word should not be above the other text.	move down	This word should not be above the other text.
Move text left to lessen indention.	move text left 5 spaces	Move text left to lessen indention.
Move text to the right to make a hanging indent.	move right	Move text to right to make a hanging indent.

We will go to the mall if her mother says she can go.	move copy as shown	If her mother says she can go, we will go to the mall.
Check the logbook. The production rate should be shown.	run on (join elements) no paragraph.	Check the logbook. The production rate should be shown.
SS ⌐ Minutes should be single spaced.	single space	Minutes should be single spaced.
We live in the USA	spell out	We live in the United States of America.
friend	transpose	friend
The key answer is here.		The answer key is here.
The title of the book is Mary's Friend.	underline	The title of the book is Mary's Friend.

GR 5   WORD DIVISION RULES

Do **Not** Divide:

- A one syllable word or words with five or fewer characters. (Examples: planned, sprint)
- Abbreviations. (Example: YMCA)
- Contractions. (Example: isn't)
- A one-letter syllable at the beginning or end of a word. (Example: incorrect divisions: a-bout; luck-y)
- The last word on a page.

Divide Words

1. Between syllables.

   per-son-nel   rep-re-sent

38

2. After a prefix or before a suffix.
   anti-nuclear   posi-tion
   pre-register   inform-ing

3. Between two consonants when the second consonant is added with the suffix.

   submit-ting   compel-ling
   ship-ping   begin-ner

4. Between parts of a compound.

   time-sharing   work-station

5. At the hyphen between hyphenated compound words.

   self-esteem   sister-in-law

6. Between two vowels when each is sounded separately.

   evalu-ation   depreci-ation

7. Between the more logical division when the word has both a prefix and suffix.

   replace-ment (rather than re-placement)

8. After a one-letter syllable within the root of a word.

   nega-tive   apolo-gize

9. According to syllabication based upon pronunciation instead of roots and derivations.

   pre-sent (to give)   pres-ent (a gift)
   pro-ject (throw)   proj-ect (plan,
   undertaking)
   knowl-edge   chil-dren

Miscellaneous Rules

1. Do not divide between two vowels in a word when they are used to represent one sound.

   extraor-dinary   es-teemed

2. Dates may be divided between the day and year.

   November 15,—year

3. Street addresses may be divided between the street name and the words *avenue, street,* etc. If the name of the street is more than one word, the division can be made between the street names.

   11480 Fangorn—Road
   32 East—Chester Street

4. City, state and ZIP Code information may be divided between the city and state or between the state and the ZIP Code. If the city or state contains more than one word, the division can come between them.

   Orlando,—Florida 32825   Orlando, Florida—32825
   Virginia—City, VA 78651

5. Names may be divided between the first and last name. If a middle initial is used, the division comes after the initial. Avoid dividing last names unless it is absolutely necessary.

   Linda F.—Mallinson   Fitz-gerald

6. Enumerations should not be divided after the number or letter.

   You should bring the following items:—(1) notepad

7. Long titles included as part of a name may be divided between the title and the name or, if absolutely necessary, between the title.

Associate Superintendent—Roy Burns
Associate—Superintendent Roy Burns

GR 6 SPACING RULES

Abbreviations

All capital abbreviations do not require the use of periods and internal spacing except for terms such as the following:

U.S.A.	B.A.	M.S	M.A.
A.D.	B.C.	P.O.	V.P.

Small-letter abbreviations require periods but no internal spacing:

a.m.	p.m.	i.e.	Ed.D.
e.g.	e.o.m.	f.o.b.	Ph.D.

Individual's Initials

Space once after the period in the initials. However, when initials are used in a memo to signify a writer's initials, they are typed in all capitals without spaces or periods. When initials are used as reference initials they are typed in lower case without periods or spaces.

S. J. Anderson   Ms. L. Thomas-Breen

Ref. Initials: lfm   Writer's Initials: LFM

Titles

Space once after an individual's title:

Dr. Thomas Anderson   Lt. Gov. Darlene Smith

SPACING WITH PUNCTUATION MARKS

Mark	Spacing
Asterisk (*)	Do not space after an asterisk and the text that follows. Example: *Item One
Apostrophe	Do not space before or after when the apostrophe is within a word or at the end of a word.
Colon	Space twice within a sentence. Do not space before or after a colon in expressions of time. Example: 8:20 p.m.
Comma	Space once after a comma.
Dash (—)	Do not space before or after a dash.
Diagonal (/)	Do not space before or after a diagonal.
Ellipsis Marks (. . .)	Space once before and after each of the three periods within a sentence.
Enumerated Items	Single space the items and leave one blank line before and after items. Example: Bring the following items to the meeting: 1. Sales report for the last two months 2. Recommendations for award

Exclamation Point	Traditionally two spaces were left after an exclamation point at the end of a sentence. The new trend is to space once after all punctuation at the end of a sentence because software programs use proportional fonts. A quick way to change from spacing twice to once after ending sentence punctuation is to use the search and replace feature in word processing software.
Hyphen (-)	Do not space before or after a hyphen.
Parentheses	Do not space after the opening parenthesis or before the closing parenthesis. Example: (Books)
Period	Traditionally two spaces were left after a period at the end of a sentence. The new trend is to space once after all punctuation at the end of a sentence because computer software programs use proportional fonts. However, it is only in the publishing area that this change has become status quo. Brochures, annual reports, company manuals, etc., should all have one space after ending sentence punctuation. A quick way to change from spacing twice to once after ending sentence punctuation is to use the search and replace feature in word processing software.

Question Mark	Traditionally two spaces were left after a question mark at the end of a sentence. The new trend is to space once after all punctuation at the end of a sentence because computer software programs use proportional fonts. However, it is only in the publishing area that this change has become status quo. Brochures, annual reports, company manuals, etc., should all have one space after ending sentence punctuation. A quick way to change from spacing twice to once after ending sentence punctuation is to use the search and replace feature in word processing software.
Quotation Marks	Do not space after the opening quotation mark or before the closing quotation mark. Example: Tommy remarked, "I will not be home." See GP 6.5 for placement of commas and periods.
Semicolon	Space once after a semicolon.
Symbols	Space once before and after the following symbols: @ & X = Exception: if the ampersand (&) is in an all-capital abbreviation such as R&D.

GR 7 ADDRESS RULES AND GUIDELINES

Address Format for Envelope

> The preferred format for envelopes is ALL capitals, block format, and no punctuation.

Use of Abbreviations in Address

> Note: Each line of the address in an envelope should be kept to 28 keystrokes. Therefore, abbreviations may be used in the envelope address that should not be used in the inside address.

Do **Not** abbreviate the name of a city in the inside address. Abbreviate the name of the city on the envelope if the address line will be more than 28 keystrokes.

Do **Not** abbreviate the words Point, Port, Fort, Mount. (Fort Lauderdale, Florida, not Ft. Lauderdale)

Do abbreviate the word Saint in American cities. (St. Petersburg, Florida)

INSIDE AND ENVELOPE ADDRESS GUIDELINES

Item	Inside and Envelope Address (Salutation)
Addressee's title and gender are known	Use title given. If no title is given for a woman, use Ms. *Dear Ms. Whitehead*
Addressee's gender is unknown because initials are used or name doesn't denote gender	Do not use any courtesy title in address or salutation. Use the addressee's first and last name. *Leslie Anderson* *Dear Leslie Anderson:*
Addressees are husband and wife sharing same last name	Traditional: Use Mr. and Mrs. followed by the husband's first and last name. (Do not use "&" for "and.") *Mr. and Mrs. Paul Mallinson* Newer: Do not use titles. Instead use the husband's and wife's first and last names: *Jane and Paul Mallinson*
Esq., Ed.D., M.D., D.D., etc.	Do not use titles before an individual's name if an academic degree or Esq. is used: *Linda Mallinson, Ed.D.* (not Dr. Linda Mallinson, Ed.D.) *Tony Anderson, Esq.* *Margarita Viejo, M.D.*
Organizations with both men and women	Do not use Gentlemen. Use "Ladies and Gentlemen" in the salutation.

Unmarried Individuals	If the names are short enough, put them both on the first line. If they are too long to do so, put them on separate lines. *Ms. Pat Daniels and Mr. Chris Johns* 2298 Oakridge Street New York, NY 10128 or *Ms. Cassandra Strickland* *Ms. Carolyn Vandergrift* 2298 Oakridge Street New York, NY 10128 If the correspondence is informal, use only first names in the salutation. If the correspondence is formal or business related, use titles with last names in the salutation. *Dear Pat and Chris:* *Dear Ms. Daniels and Mr. Johns:*

Long job titles or company names	Indent the second and third lines of the job title or department 2 or 3 spaces:
	
	Ms. Linda Mallinson
	Executive Vice President
	    and General Manager
	National Sales Association
	1167 Basso Street
	Orlando, FL 32801
	
	Ms. Linda Mallinson
	Executive Vice President
	American Society for the Prevention
	    of Securities Fraud
	289 East Bay Street
	Washington, DC 20201

House and building numbers	Use figures for these instead of spelling out the number including house and building names using 2-10. The number 1 is spelled out to avoid confusion. Do not use the # symbol or the abbreviation No.: *One* Anderson Place 4 Park Avenue 76 Basso Lane
Numbers used as street names	Spell out numbers 1-10: 1176 *Fourth* Avenue Use figures for numbers above 10 followed by *st, nd, rd,* or *th*. 234 *59th* Street
Compass points (East, West, South-east, North-west, etc.) appearing **before** the street name	1. Do <u>not</u> abbreviate compass point unless the street address is very long: 932 *Northeast* Elm Road (Note: The United States Postal Service prefers the compass point to be abbreviated on the envelope.) *932 NE Elm Street* 2. If the compass point is part of the city name, do not abbreviate it. *West Palm Beach, FL 32818*

Compass points (East, West, Southeast, Northwest, etc.) appearing **after** the street name	Abbreviate **compound** directions (NE, NW, SE, SW). Insert a comma before the abbreviations and do not use periods: 870 22nd Street, *SW* Spell out **North, South, East, and West**. Do not use commas: 9 Anderson Drive *South* (Note: The United States Postal Service prefers the compass point to be abbreviated on the envelope.) 9 Anderson Drive *S*
ZIP Codes	Although two spaces between the two letter state abbreviation and the ZIP Code is still preferred by the United States Postal Service, it is now acceptable to space only once after the state abbreviation. Orlando, *FL 32825*
Post office box numbers	Use either a post office box number or street address. Do not include both in address. Use the Post Office Box number for regular mail and the street address for Express Mail. Any of the following formats may be used: Post Box 976 P.O. Box 976 PO Box 976 *(Note: The United States Postal Service prefers the all capital abbreviation PO BOX to be used on the envelope. Notice no periods are used in the abbreviation.)*

PLACEMENT OF MAILING PARTS IN AN ADDRESS

Address Part	Placement
Attention line (See DF 4 and DF 18) See Figure 3	On the envelope and inside address the attention line should be typed as the first line of the address: *Attn Mr. Paul Anderson* Marine Enterprises, Inc. 1087 Main St. Richmond, VA 22042-1441 It is not necessary to include an attention line in the letter. An "organizational" salutation such as "Ladies and Gentlemen" should be used.
Building Name	Place the name of a building on the line above the street or PO Box. Ms. Ann Thibodeau Central Florida Enterprises *Delta Tower Plaza* Rm 108 56 Sylvan Blvd. Orlando, FL 32825
Department or Division	Place the name of the department or division above the name of the company. Ms. Linda Mallinson, Manager *Department of International Sales* BankAmerica Corp. 1167 Basso Street Cincinnati, OH 32801

	The U.S. Postal Service <u>prefers</u> for the apartment or suite to be printed at the end of the delivery address. An acceptable alternative is on the line immediately above the street address line.
Apartment, Building, Suite, or Room Numbers	Do **not** include abbreviations or symbols such as No. or #. If a building number is included, place it on the line with the building name.
Common Abbreviations (See GR 9 for more) Apt. Bldg. FL (floor) Ste (Suite) Unit Rm (Room) Dept.	Ms. Ann Thibodeau Central Florida Enterprises Delta Tower Plaza *Rm 108* 56 Sylvan Blvd. Orlando, FL 32825 Dr. Linda Mallinson 11870 Sanborn Road *Apt. 101* Orlando, FL 32825 or Dr. Bernice Muroski-Palowitch *Apt. 101* 1870 Sanborn Road Orlando, FL 32825 Dr. Bernice Muroski-Palowitch Nations Finance 1356 Executive Dr. *Ste 202* Orlando, FL 32825 or Dr. Bernice Muroski-Palowitch Nations Finance *Ste 202* *1356 Executive Dr.* *Orlando, FL 32825* *Dr. Bernice Muroski-Palowitch* *1600 Central PL Bldg. 14* *Orlando, FL 32825*

In Care of	Place the In Care Of (c/o) notation on the line after the person to whom the letter is addressed. Ms. Linda Mallinson *c/o Mr. Raymond DeChant* 398 Oak Ridge Road Orlando, FL 32809
Job titles	Place an individual's job title on the line below his or her name, or if the job title is short, it may be placed after the individual's name: Ms. Linda Mallinson *Director of Research* National Sales Association 1167 Basso Street Orlando, FL 32801 Ms. Linda Mallinson, *Manager* National Sales Association 1167 Basso Street Orlando, FL 32801
Mail stop codes	Put a mail stop code on the **first** line of the address abbreviated MSC: *MSC 287* Ms. Linda Mallinson, Manager National Sales Association 1167 Basso Street Orlando, FL 32801
Post Office Box	The Post Box Number replaces the street address: Mr. Janet MacPherson TV Production Department Random House International *PO Box 2976* Indianapolis, IN 46205

GR 8 TWO-LETTER STATE ABBREVIATIONSFOR U.S. MAIL

Note: Use these abbreviations only in addresses. When abbreviating state names in other situations, use the traditional state abbreviation.

Alabama	AL
Alaska	AK
Arizona	AZ
Arkansas	AR
California	CA
Colorado	CO
Connecticut	CT
Delaware	DE
District of Columbia	DC
Florida	FL
Georgia	GA
Guam	GU
Hawaii	HI
Idaho	ID
Illinois	IL
Indiana	IN
Iowa	IA
Kansas	KS
Kentucky	KY
Louisiana	LA
Maine	ME
Maryland	MD
Massachusetts	MA
Michigan	MI
Minnesota	MN
Mississippi	MS
Missouri	MO
Montana	MT
Nebraska	NE
Nevada	NV
New Hampshire	NH
New Jersey	NJ

New Mexico	NM
New York	NY
North Carolina	NC
North Dakota	ND
Ohio	OH
Oklahoma	OK
Oregon	OR
Pennsylvania	PA
Puerto Rico	PR
Rhode Island	RI
South Carolina	SC
South Dakota	SD
Tennessee	TN
Texas	TX
Utah	UT
Vermont	VT
Virgin Islands	VI
Virginia	VA
Washington	WA
West Virginia	WV
Wisconsin	WI
Wyoming	WY

GR 9   ABBREVIATIONS USED IN STREET ADDRESSES

These are some address abbreviations. *Avoid using these abbreviations in inside addresses.* It is acceptable, however, to use them on envelopes. The U.S. Postal Service lists abbreviations for cities, towns, places, streets, roads, etc., in the ZIP Code Directory.

Administration	ADMN
Agent	AGNT
Annex	ANX
Apartment	APT
Association	ASSN
Attorney	ATTY

Avenue	AVE
Beach	BCH
Bookkeeping	BKPG
Boulevard	BLVD
Branch	BR
Building	BLDG
Center(s)	CTR
Central	CTRL
Chairman	CHRMN
Circle	CIR
Commander	CMDR
Company	CO
Courts	CTS
Crescent	CRES
Department	DEPT
Drive	DR
East	E
Expressway	EXPY
Fort	FT
Freeway	FWY
Government	GOVT
Height(s)	HTS
Highway	HWY
Institute	INST
Island	IS
Junction	JCT
Lake	LK
Lakes	LKS
Lane	LN
Manager	MGR
Mount	MT
Mountain	MTN
Northeast	NE
Northwest	NW
Parkway	PKY
Place	PL
Plaza	PLZ
Port	PRT

Post Office	PO
President	PRES
River	RIV
Road(s)	RD
Room	RM.
Route	RT
Rural Route	RR
Saint	ST
Shore	SHR
Southeast	SE
Southwest	SW
Square	SQ
Station	STA
Street(s)	PST
Terrace	TER
Township	TWNSHP
Union	UN
Upper	UPR
Turnpike	TPKE
Valley(s)	VLY
Vice President	VP
View	VW
Village	VLG
West	W

GR 10 SPELLING OF COMMON CITIES IN THE UNITED STATES

Following are names of cities in the United States that may be difficult to spell because they are not necessarily spelled the way they are pronounced. Names of many cities can be found in several states. For instance, Savannah is a city in Missouri as well as in Georgia; Montgomery is a city in Ohio and Alabama; Syracuse is a city in Nebraska as well as in New York. The state(s) given is for the state(s) in which the city is most widely known.

CITY	STATE
Akron	Ohio, Colorado
Albany	New York
Albuquerque	New Mexico
Anaheim	California
Anchorage	Alaska
Annapolis	Maryland
Aspen	Colorado
Augusta	Georgia
Aurora	Colorado
Austin	Texas
Baltimore	Maryland
Bangor	Maine
Baton Rouge	Louisiana
Birmingham	Alabama
Bismarck	North Dakota
Boise	Idaho
Charlotte	North Carolina
Chattanooga	Tennessee
Cheyenne	Colorado, Wyoming
Cincinnati	Ohio
Cleveland	Ohio
Corpus Christi	Texas
Decatur	Georgia, Illinois, Alabama
Des Moines	Iowa
Des Plaines	Illinois
Detroit	Michigan
Devonshire	Connecticut
El Paso	Texas
Eugene	Oregon
Eureka	California
Fayetteville	North Carolina
Frankfort	Louisiana
Fremont	California
Fresno	California
Gainesville	Florida
Geneva	Michigan
Greensboro	North Carolina

Greenwich Village	New York
Hialeah	Florida
Honolulu	Hawaii
Indianapolis	Indiana
Juneau	Alaska
Kalamazoo	Michigan
Ketchikan	Alaska
Knoxville	Tennessee
Los Angeles	California
Louisville	Kentucky
Lubbock	Texas
Madison	Wisconsin
Malibu	California
Manhattan	New York
Maui	Hawaii
Memphis	Tennessee
Mesa	Arizona
Milwaukee	Wisconsin
Minneapolis	Minnesota
Mobile	Alabama
Monterey	California
Montgomery	Alabama
Monticello	Virginia
Montpelier	Vermont
Murfreesboro	Arkansas, Tennessee
Nashville	Tennessee
Newark	New Jersey
Newport News	Virginia
Niagara Falls	New York
Nome	Alaska
Norfolk	Virginia
Oklahoma City	Oklahoma
Omaha	Nebraska
Peoria	Illinois
Philadelphia	Pennsylvania
Phoenix	Arizona
Piedmont	Virginia
Pierre	South Dakota
Pittsburgh	Pennsylvania

Poughkeepsie	New York
Providence	Rhode Island
Pueblo	Colorado
Raleigh	North Carolina
Roanoke	Virginia
Rochester	New York
Sacramento	California
Salem	Ohio
San Antonio	Texas
San Diego	California
San Francisco	California
San Jose	California
Santa Ana	California
Savannah	Georgia
Schenectady	New York
Secaucus	New Jersey
Seattle	Washington
Shreveport	Louisiana
Sioux	Nebraska
Sitka	Alaska
Sommersville	Connecticut
Spokane	Washington
Suffolk	Virginia
Syracuse	New York
Tacoma	Washington
Tallahassee	Florida
Tok	Alaska
Toledo	Ohio
Topeka	Kansas
Tucson	Arizona
Tulsa	Oklahoma
Tuscaloosa	Alabama
Wichita	Kansas
Yonkers	New York
Ypsilanti	Michigan

GR 11 ADDRESSING INTERNATIONAL MAIL

GR 11.1 GENERAL GUIDELINES

Item	Guidelines
Correspondence originating from the United States to someone outside of the United States	Spell out the country name and place it in all capitals as the last line of the address: Mr. Kevin Hamilton 56 Muir Street East Toronto, Ontario *CANADA* Mr. Kevin Hamilton Happy Family Hostel Taipei, Taiwan *REPUBLIC OF CHINA*
Correspondence originating from a country outside of the United States to someone in the United States	Spell out United States of America and place it in all capitals as the last line of the address: Ms. Linda Mallinson Vice President and General Manager National Sales 1167 Basso Street Orlando, FL 32801 UNITED STATES OF AMERICA

GR 11.2 COMMON INTERNATIONAL PROVINCES AND CITIES

Argentina
- Buenos Aires

Australia
- Sydney

Brazil
- Bahia
- Sao Paul
- Rio de Janeiro

Canada (See GR 11.5)

China
- Biijing (Peking)
- Chengdu
- Guangzhou (Canton)
- Nanjing (Nanking)
- Shanghai
- Shenyang
- Tianjin (Tienstin)
- Xian

Denmark
- Copenhagen

Egypt
- Cairo

Germany
- Frankfurt
- Munich-Riem

India
- Ahmedabad
- Bangalore
- Bombay
- Calcutta
- Delhi
- Hyderabad
- Jaipur
- Madras
- Nagpur
- Pune (Poona)

Indonesia
- Jakarta

Israel
- Tel Aviv
- Jaffa
- Jerusalem
- Haifa

Italy
- Bologna
- Firenze (Florence)
- Genova (Genoa)
- Milano (Milan)
- Napoli (Naples)
- Roma (Rome)
- Torino (Turin)
- Venezia (Venice)

Japan
- Fukuoka
- Hiroshima
- Kawasaki
- Kitakyushu
- Kobe
- Kyoto
- Nagoya
- Osaka
- Sapporo
- Sendai
- Tokyo
- Yokohama

Korea
- Inchon (Incheon)
- Kwangju
- Pusan (Busan)
- Seoul
- Taegu
- Taejon

Mexico
- Acapulco
- Cancún
- Guadalajara
- Estado de México
- Chihuahua
- México
- Monterrey
- Puerto Vallarto
- Taegu
- Taejon Puebla
- Torreon
- Tijuana
- Cd. Juárez

Netherlands
- Amsterdam
- Apeldoorn
- Arnhem
- Eindhoven
- Groningen
- Den Ahaag
- Haarlem
- Rotterdam
- Utrecht

Norway
- Oslo

Russia
- Moscow
- Vladivostok

Saudi Arabia
- Riyadh (the Capital)
- Jeddah
- Dhahran
- Jubail
- Yanbu

Spain
- Badajoz
- Barcelona
- Bilbao
- Granada
- Madrid
- Murcia
- San Sebastián
- Servilla
- Valencia

Sweden
- Stockholm
- Malmö
- Göteborg
  (Gothenburg)

Switzerland
- Geneva
- Lausanne
- Basel
- Bern (Berne)
- Zürich

Taiwan
- Taipei (the Capital)
- Kaohsiung
- Keelung
- Tainan

- **Thailand**
- Bangkok

**United Kingdom
(England, Wales
Scotland, Ireland)**
- Aberdeen
- Bath
- Belfast
- Birmingham
- Brighton
- Bristol
- Cambridge
- Chester
- Coventry
- Dublin
- Dundee
- Edinburgh
- Exeter
- Glasgow
- Gloucester
- Ipswich
- Killarney
- Leicester
- Liverpool
- London
- Manchester
- Nottingham
- Norwich
- Oldham
- Oxford
- Sheffield

New Zealand
- Auckland

GR 11.3   SPECIAL CHARACTERS

Many foreign words have national characters, which use accents and diacritical marks. In order to compose these characters, specific keystrokes are used. The following information describes how to create these characters using popular software programs.

WordPerfect for Windows

- Choose Insert
- Choose Character or press the CTRL and W keys at the same time. This displays the WordPerfect characters dialog box.
- Choose the Multinational set of characters from the Character Set pop-up list.
- Scroll down to see the letters with the symbols over them. Double click on the desired character to insert it.

Microsoft Word (Macintosh)

- Insert
- Symbol
- Select "Normal Text" from "Font" Pop Up Options
- Double click on the character or symbol to insert it

Microsoft Word (Windows)

- Insert
- Symbol
- Select "Normal Text" from "Font" Pop Up Options or select the name of a specific font
- Double click on the character with symbol to insert it

GR 11.4 GENERAL ADDRESS REQUIREMENTS

- The bottom line of the address should show only the country in all capitals with no abbreviations.

- Do not put the postal codes (ZIP Codes) of the foreign country on the last line of the address (unless the mail is going to Canada; See GP 11.5).

- Do not underline the country name.

```
DOROTHY  DIETRIC-RSICHER
MANNSTRASSEE 7
5300 BONN 1
GERMANY
```

GR 11.5   CANADIAN MAIL

Canada is divided into two territories and ten provinces. Although Canadians use lower case in addressing mail domestically, the city name should be written in all capitals without punctuation when mail is addressed from **outside** of Canada. Example:

Calgary AB	Edmonton AB
Halifax NS	Montreal PQ
Ottawa ON	Regina SK
Toronto ON	Vancouver BC
Winnipeg MB	

Example:

Ms. Jane MacAllister	Title, Given Name, Family Name
International Publishing Ltd.	Ltd. (Limited) = Corporation
249 Adelaide St., Suite 203	Bldg. #, Street Name, Suite
TORONTO, ON M5A 1N1	City, 2-ltr. Province Abbr., 6
CANADA	character postcode

Notice as shown in the following examples that it is optional to place delivery postal zones in the last line of the address in Canadian mail.

```
MS REBECCA BERCHERTZ
890 APEX STREET
OTTAWA  ON K1A OB1
CANADA
```

or

```
MS REBECCA BERCHERTZ
890 APEX STREET
OTTAWA  ON CANADA
K1A  OB1
```

65

Example of a Canadian French-language street address:

Address	Explanation Code #
Mr. Jean-Louis Macon	1
Èditions Internationales Ltée.	2
1803 rue Notre-Dame O., bur. 843	3
Case Postale 1123	4
Montréal, PQ H3A 2T7	5
CANADA	

Code Explanation

1) Title, Given name, Family name
2) Ltée. Signifies corporation
3) Building No., rue = street (no initial capital),
   O = abbreviation for Ouest meaning West,
   bur. = bureau meaning room or suite
4) Case Postale means "P.O. Box"
5) City, Postcode for the box number

Canadian Postal Abbreviations

Although it is acceptable to abbreviate the name of the province or territory in a Canadian address, the Canada Post Office prefers the unabbreviated form.

Alberta	AB
British Columbia	BC
Labrador	LB
Manitoba	MB
New Brunswick	NB
Newfoundland	NF
Northwest Territories	NT
Nova Scotia	NS
Ontario	ON
Prince Edward Island	PE
Quebec	PQ, QC
Saskatchewan	SK
Yukon Territory	YT

GR 11.6 PUERTO RICAN MAIL

The word CALLE (Spanish for street) or AVENIDA (Spanish for avenue) is placed before the street name and number. Below are examples of common formats for addressing mail to Puerto Rico.

Place the house number <u>before</u> the street name.

MR. JUAN VALDEZ	Name
150 JULIO ENRIQUE VIZCARRONDO	Street Address
CAGUAS PR 00725-1103	City, State, ZIP

MR. JUAN VALDEZ	Name
RES LAS MARGARITAS	Residential Name
EDIF 1 APT 104	Building No. and Apt. No.
CAGUAS PR 00725-1103	City, State, and ZIP + 4

MR RALPH PEREZ	Name
COND GARDEN HILLS PL	Condominium Name
TORRE 2 APT 905	Building No. and Apt. No.
GUYANABO PR 00966-2325	City, State, and ZIP + 4

Common Translations for Phrases in Puerto Rico addresses:

Spanish	English and Abbreviations
Apartado	PO Box
Buzon	Box
Buzon Rural	Rural Box
Ruta Rural	Rural Route
Ruta Estrella	Highway Contract
Edificio	Building
Apartamento	APT
Barriada	BDA
Building	BLDG
Departamento	DEPT
Edificio	EDIF
Hospital	HOSP

Residencial	RES
Norte	North
Noreste	Northeast
Noroeste	Northwest
Sur	South
Sureste	Southeast

GR 11.7   MILITARY MAIL

Typical Delivery Address for military mail is standardized as follows:

Psc (Command or Unit) Name
Box Number or Ship's Name

Examples:

SSGT RANDY KLINE UNIT 2089 BOX 1965 APO AP 95673-9276	SGT BARRY WETZEL USCGC HAMILTON FPO AP 96667-3931

GR 12: TIME ZONES

A good resource on current time zones is

http://www.worldtimeserver.com

UNITED STATES TIME ZONES

The following chart shows the differences between the time zones in the United States and what states are in specific time zones.

*The following states have "special" time zone features where different parts of the state are in different time zones:

Florida, Idaho, Indiana, Kansas, Kentucky, Michigan, Nebraska, North Dakota, Oregon, North Dakota, Oregon, South Dakota, Tennessee, and Texas.

Alaska	Hawaii	Pacific PST	Mountain MDT	Central CST	Eastern EST
7 a.m.	7 a.m.	9 a.m.	10 a.m.	11 a.m.	noon
		• CA • NV • OR* • WA	• AZ • CO • ID* • MT • NM • UT • WY	• AL • IA • IL • KS* • KY* • LA • MN • MO • MS • ND* • NE* • OK • SD* • TN* • TX* • WI	• FL* • GA • IN* • KY • *MI • NC • NY • OH • PA • SC • TN • VI • WV

GR 13: TIME DIFFERENCES

The following chart shows the time differences between some countries.

Country	TIME ZONE			
	Pacific PDT	Mountain MDT	Central CST	Eastern EST
Argentina	+2	+3	+4	+5
Australia (Sydney)	+15	+16	+17	+18
Austria	+6	+7	+8	+9
Belgium	+6	+7	+8	+9
Bolivia	+1	+2	+3	+4
Brazil	+2	+3	+4	+5
Chile	+1	+2	+3	+4
Colombia	+0	+1	+2	+3
Costa Rica	-1	+0	+1	+2
Denmark	+6	+7	+8	+9
Equador	+0	+1	+2	+3
El Salvador	-1	+0	+1	+2
England	See United Kingdom			
Finland	+7	+8	+9	+10
France	+6	+7	+8	+9
France	+6	+7	+8	+9
Germany	+6	+7	+8	+9
Greece	+7	+8	+9	+10
Guatemala	-1	+0	+1	+2
Haiti	+0	+1	+2	+3
Honduras	-1	+0	+1	+2
Hong Kong	+13	+14	+15	+16
Indonesia	+12	+13	+14	+15
Iran	+8 1/2	+9 1/2	+10 1/2	+11 1/2
Iraq	+8	+9	+10	+11
Ireland	+5	+6	+7	+8
Israel	+7	+8	+9	+10
Italy	+6	+7	+8	+9

Country	TIME ZONE			
	Pacific PDT	Mountain MDT	Central CST	Eastern EST
Japan	+14	+15	+16	+17
Kenya	+8	+9	+10	+11
Korea	+14	+15	+16	+17
Libya	+7	+8	+9	+10
Luxembourg	+6	+7	+8	+9
Malaysia	+13	+14	+15	+16
Monaco	+6	+7	+8	+9
Netherlands	+6	+7	+8	+9
New Zealand	+17	+18	+19	+20
Nicaragua	-1	+0	+1	+2
Nigeria	+6	+7	+8	+9
Norway	+6	+7	+8	+9
Panama	+0	+1	+2	+3
Paraguay	+1	+2	+3	+4
Peru	+0	+1	+2	+3
Philippines	+13	+14	+15	+16
Portugal	+5	+6	+7	+8
Romania	+7	+8	+9	+10
Russia	+8	+9	+10	+11
Saudi Arabia	+8	+9	+10	+11
Singapore	+13	+14	+15	+16
South Africa	+7	+8	+9	+10
Spain	+6	+7	+8	+9
Sweden	+6	+7	+8	+9
Switzerland	+6	+7	+8	+9
Tahiti	-5	-4	-3	-2
Taiwan	+13	+14	+15	+16
Thailand	+12	+13	+14	+15
Turkey	+8	+9	+10	+11
United Kingdom	+5	+6	+7	+8
Venezuela	+1	+2	+3	+4

GRAMMAR AND PUNCTUATION

GLOSSARY OF GRAMMAR TERMS

Adjectives	Words that describe nouns and pronouns. Answer questions such as: What kind? How many? Which ones? (Example: big, several, oldest)
Adverbs	Words that give additional information about a verb, another adverb, or adjective. Adverbs answer: In what manner? Where? When? and to what extent? (Example: here, now, carefully, sharply, too)
Antecedent	The word or words that personal pronouns refer to or replace.
Appositives	Nouns that explain or rename other nouns. (Example: Riley's first book, _Liberty First,_ was his best seller.)
Clause	A group of words in a sentence that has both a subject and a predicate. Clauses don't always express a complete thought.
Common Noun	Refers to general names of people, places, things, activities, or ideas. (Example: girl)
Conjunction	Words that connect two or more words or two parts of a sentence. (Examples: and, or, nor)

Coordinating Conjunction	Conjunctions that join equal parts (words, phrases, or clauses) of a sentence. (Examples: We ordered staples <u>and</u> computer disks. We paid for the supplies <u>and</u> left the film to be processed. I order all the department's computer supplies, <u>and</u> I keep an inventory of supplies on hand.)
Correlative Conjunctions	Conjunctions used in pairs to join related parts of a sentence. (Examples: both, and; either, or; neither, nor; not, but; not only, but also)
Dependent Clause	A clause that cannot stand by itself as a sentence and depends on another clause to complete its meaning. (Example: <u>When the new computers arrive</u>, we will have to transfer to the new accounting system.)
Dependent or Subor-dinating Conjunctions	Conjunctions that join unequal parts of a sentence such as an independent and dependent clause. (Example: <u>If</u> I study hard, I should make the honor roll. I am not interested in purchasing clothes on the Internet <u>because</u> I like to make sure clothes fit before I buy them.)

Future Verb Tense	Verbs that show action that will take place in the future. Most future tense verbs use "will" or "shall." (Example: will run, will succeed) Some future tense verbs use "will be" or "shall be." (Examples: will be running, will have taken, shall be done)
Gerund	A verb form ending in "ing" that is used as a noun. (Example: <u>Fishing in Canada</u> is Jerry's idea of a perfect vacation.)
Helping Verbs	Verbs that come before a main verb to complete the verb. (Examples: were, been, shall, have, has, had, do, does, might, would, are, is, etc.)
Indefinite Pronouns	Pronouns that do not refer to one specific person or thing. (Examples: somebody, every, each, anybody, no one, etc.)
Independent Clause	A clause that expresses a complete thought. (Example: When the new computers arrive, <u>we will have to transfer to the new accounting system.</u>)
Infinitive	The present part of a verb plus the word "to."
Infinitive Phrase	The infinitive (<u>to</u> and a verb) and its modifiers.

Interjections	Words that show emotion or a strong reaction. (Examples: Ouch, oh, wow, oops)
Linking Verbs	Verbs that do not show action but show a "state of being." They are used to link parts of a sentence. (Example: am, is, are, was, were, been, being, etc.)
Nouns	Words that name people, places, things, activities, or ideas. (Examples: boy, United States, cups, softball, design)
Parenthetical Expression	A group of words that can be removed from a sentence without changing its meaning. Parenthetical expressions can be nonessential words or phrases, direct addresses, or appositives.
Participial Phrase	Phrase that begins with a verb form that is used as an adjective.
Past Participle	Verbal formed by adding "ed" or "d" preceded by a helping verb or verbs. (Example: Having finished with the project, Karen relaxed and read a novel.)

Past Verb Tense	Verbs that show action that happened in the past. Usually adding "ed" forms past tense (Examples: used, danced, placed, chased) The past tense of some verbs require changing the verb form itself. (Example: (took, came, ran, swam, had, did, brought, taught, flew, gave). To show past tense as seen from the present, use "has" or "have" with the past tense. (Examples: has liked, has printed, have baked, has skied, have run, has given, has flown, have taught, has swum)
Personal Pronouns	Substitute for nouns referring to people. (Examples: I me, my, mine, you, your, he, she, it, him, her, they, them, our, etc.)
Phrase	A group of related words that don't have either a subject or predicate. Phrases can act as nouns, verbs, adjectives, or adverbs. (Examples: Selling the most goods (noun); Jon should have been (verb); on the top shelf (adverb, preposition); of the company (adjective, preposition)

Possessive Pronouns	Pronouns that show ownership. (Examples: my, mine, our, his, her)
Predicate	The predicate of a sentence is its verb or verbs and all the modifiers that describe the verb(s). (Examples: The school <u>awards degrees in business and art.</u> Community members <u>are excellent role models and student mentors.</u>)
Preposition	Words that connect nouns or pronouns to other words in a sentence. (Examples: about, above, across, after, into, past, up, upon, from, for, in, during, down, behind, etc.)
Prepositional Phrase	A phrase that begins with a preposition and ends with a noun or pronoun. The ending noun or pronoun in the prepositional phrase is called the "object of the preposition" and can never be the subject of a sentence. (Examples: of the boxes; on the shelf)

Present Participle	Verb tense used to describe something that is continuing. It can be action currently taking place, action that was going on in the past, or action that will go on in the future. Formed by adding "ing" to the verb. Differs from a gerund in that it does not act as a noun or subject of a sentence. It acts as an adjective. (Examples: <u>Having difficulty following the directions</u>, I asked Fred to put the stereo together. <u>Reading the manual and using the online help</u>, Mary taught herself Microsoft Word.)
Present Verb Tense	Verbs that show action taking place in the present. Many present tense verbs include "s" at the end. (Examples: does, runs, talks, walks, has) Some present tense verbs add "ing" or "ing" with a helping verb. (Examples: is running, am talking, walking)
Pronouns	Words that take the place nouns. (Examples: she, he, it, we, I, you, they, his, their, her, your)
Proper Noun	Refers to a specific person, place, thing, activity, or idea. (Example: Florida)

Subject	The noun or pronoun being discussed in the sentence. The part of a sentence that tells "who is speaking," "who is spoken to," or "who or what is spoken about."
Transitional Conjunctions	Conjunctions that make a transition between two equal parts of a sentence. (Examples: accordingly, additionally, also, hence, however, incidentally, indeed, in fact, thus, therefore, meanwhile, moreover, consequently, then, nevertheless, otherwise, still, for example, besides, furthermore)
Verbal	A participle, gerund, or infinitive that contains a verb form but functions as a noun, adjective, or adverb.
Verbs	Words that show action (Examples: caught, ran, played, slept) or state of being (Examples: am, is, are).

GP 1 PERIODS

Periods are used at the end of declarative sentences. A declarative sentence is a sentence that makes a statement. (She went to school early.)

Question marks are used at the end of a sentence that asks a question. (Who turned out the lights?)

84

GP 1.1 REQUESTS

Periods are used instead of question marks when the question asked is a courteous request. Courteous requests do not require a "yes or no" response. Instead they require action.

If you can't complete the report by the deadline, could you please let Mary know.

Would you please keep this matter confidential.

GP 1.2 LISTS

Use a period after each item in a list if it is used to complete the sentence introducing the list. For instance, if the introductory stem ends in a prepositional phrase, periods should be placed after the items in the list.

We will purchase equipment in:

Canada.
Italy.
Spain.

Do not use a period after items in a list if the sentence is complete (stem does not end with a preposition).

Please review the following items before the meeting:

Last year's tax audit
Last year's earnings record
This year's budget proposal

GP 2   QUESTION MARK

GP 2.1 SERIES

Use question marks in place of commas when a series of questions is used. Space once after these internal question marks.

> Is Mary prepared for the new position? lower salary? more responsibility?

GP 3   COMMAS

GP 3.1 COMPOUND SENTENCES

Use a comma before coordinate conjunctions (and, but, for, so, or, yet, nor) that connect two independent clauses of a compound sentence. (Hint: To determine if the sentence is compound and if a comma is needed, see if a sentence is on either side of the conjunction. If so, a comma is needed before the conjunction.)

Exception: If the independent clauses on either side of the conjunction are four words or less, do not use a comma.

> The administrators met to discuss the cost-of-living increase, but they did not come to a decision. *(Compound sentence. Clauses on either side of "but" can stand as separate sentences; therefore, a comma is needed.)*
>
> The supervisor and office manager checked the letter.
> *(Not a compound sentence. The clauses on either side of "and" can't stand as separate sentences; therefore, no comma is needed.)*
>
> Ask for Saturday off and I will too.
> *(The clauses on either side of "and" can stand as separate sentences, but they are only four words.)*

GP 3.2 PHRASES AND CLAUSES

Place a comma after an introductory phrase and after an introductory dependent clause.

GP 3.2A PREPOSITIONAL PHRASES

Place a comma after a prepositional phrase <u>used to introduce a sentence</u>. Some common prepositions are:

about	between	over
above	beyond	past
across	by	regarding
after	concerning	since
against	down	through
along	during	throughout
among	except	to
around	for	toward
as	from	under
at	in	until
before	into	up
behind	like	upon
below	of	with
beneath	off	within
beside	on	without

> *At the association's last meeting*, a new chairperson was elected.
>
> *Since she was a recent graduate*, she decided to take a break from school and work to tour the country.

- **Do not place a comma before a prepositional phrase <u>at the end of a sentence</u> unless it is NOT essential to the meaning of the sentence.**

> She decided to take a break from school and work to tour the country for six months.

87

- **Do not put a comma after a preposition that refers to time or place (tells when, how often, or where).**

At the downtown library students can use computers to access the Internet. *(No comma–tells where)*

On October 3 we will switch to the new system. *(No comma–tells when)*

GP 3.2B PARTICIPIAL PHRASES

Participial phrases are phrases that begin with a verb form used as an adjective.

Always set off participial phrases with commas.

Having worked for the company for one year, John was eligible for a promotion.

Pitfall	Example:
Do not confuse a participial phrase with a gerund phrase. A gerund phrase begins with a gerund (a verb form ending in "ing" that is used as a noun and is the subject of the sentence). Never use commas to set off gerund phrases.	Controlling the cost of internal communications is one of the administrator's jobs. Gerund Phrase *Controlling the cost of internal communications* is the <u>subject</u> of the sentence. No comma is needed.

GP 3.2C   INFINITIVE PHRASES

Infinitive phrases begin with "to" plus a verb.

Always set off infinitive phrases with commas <u>if they are not the subject of the sentence</u>.

To understand the organization of the company, the new employee should refer to the organizational chart. (Infinitive phrase is <u>not</u> used as the subject of the sentence so a comma is needed.)

To become an advertising manager is his goal. (No comma is needed because the infinitive phrase <u>is</u> the subject of the sentence.)

GP 3.2D   DEPENDENT CLAUSES

The following are words that frequently begin a dependent clause.

After	Inasmuch as
Although	No matter what
As	So that
As if	Though
As long as	Unless
As soon as	Until
As though	When
Because	Whenever
Even though	Whereas
If	Wherever
In order that	While

Always set off introductory dependent clauses with a comma.

When the mail arrives in the morning, it must be sorted by departments.

If we had planned better, we would have had time to take an earlier flight.

- **If the dependent clause comes at the end of the sentence, no comma is usually needed. The only time a comma is needed is if the clause is NOT essential to the sentence.**

Ashley did not accept the job offer because she thought she would get a promotion.

GP 3.3   NONESSENTIAL PHRASES

GP 3.3A   PARENTHETICAL PHRASES

A **parenthetical phrase** or clause is <u>not necessary</u> to the meaning of the sentence and should be set off by commas. The position of the phrase in the sentence does not matter. (Hint: If the sentence can be read without the expression and still maintain its meaning and clarity, it is unnecessary and should be set off with commas.)

Which and That

When considering if a phrase is essential or not, the following guideline helps with the words "which" and "that":

Which indicates text that is <u>not</u> essential to the sentence. A comma is required.

That indicates text that <u>is</u> essential to the sentence. No comma should be used.

Since he is MOUS certified, Marty should be familiar with the Microsoft curriculum, which was ordered last week.

He should be able to take advantage of the transfer that will become available in June.

The words below are common parenthetical expressions that often require commas because they introduce nonessential information.

As a consequence	In fact
As a matter of fact	In my opinion
As you know	Of course
For instance	On the contrary
However	Unfortunately

He was, *in my opinion*, a very hard worker.

However, the passing score on the employment test was 75.

The passing score on the employment test, *however*, was 75.

However important the recommendation letter is to the application process, it must be supported by the transcripts and tests. (Note: no comma is used after "however" because it is needed for clarity.)

The current rate of inflation is expected to continue for at least three months, *so the government advisors say.*

Mr. Peterson, *who used to be in advertising,* has joined our production team.

Such As and Etc.

When "such as" introduces nonessential information, use a comma before but not after "such as." If the "such as" phrase is essential to the sentence, no commas should be used.

A comma should always be used before and after "etc." unless it is at the end of the sentence.

Some of the staff, such as Jane and Tim, will receive additional computer training.

Phrases such as "raining cats and dogs" and "when it rains it pours" confuse students who are learning to speak English. *(Commas should not be used because the "such as" phrase tells what types of phrases are confusing. The phrase is essential to the sentence.)*

The camp brochure covered information about arrival time, insurance, clothing, transportation, closing ceremonies, refund policy, etc.

GP 3.3B   CONTRASTING EXPRESSIONS

Contrasting expressions are phrases that often begin with *but only, not,* and *rather than* that are not essential to the meaning of the sentence. Put a comma after contrasting nonessential expressions.

Rather than be late to class, she stayed home.

The supervisor changed the employees' workdays, but not their hours, for the next month.

Ms. Royal was able to sell her house, but only after she had it on the market for a year.

GP 3.3C TRANSITIONAL EXPRESSIONS

See GP 4.3 for rules concerning using semicolons with transitional expressions.

Transitional expressions are parenthetical expressions that carry the thought from one sentence or paragraph to another and help the reader relate the thoughts. Some common transitional expressions are:

accordingly	consequently	likewise
additionally	finally	meanwhile
after all	first of all	moreover
afterward	for example	namely
all things considered	for the most part	next
also	furthermore	now
anyway	generally	of course
as a result	hence	ordinarily
as a rule	however	otherwise
as usual	in addition	rather
at any rate	in any case	second
at first	in conclusion	similarly
besides	in essence	still
briefly	in other words	therefore
by and large	in short	thus
by contrast	in the long run	usually
by the same token	in time	
by the way	instead	

Put commas after transitional expressions.

After all, he had the highest sales in the department.

Consequently, he should get the raise.

It is extremely urgent, *therefore,* that you contact him immediately.

Sara, *likewise*, qualified for the raise.

GP 3.4 APPOSITIONS

Separate an element in apposition (word, phrase, or clause that provides further information) when it is **not** needed. This rule applies no matter where the apposition is placed in the sentence. Hint: When a noun is <u>not</u> identified, the word, phrase, or clause that follows it is necessary.

Phrases and clauses beginning with *this, these, those, which,* and *such as* are usually set off with commas.

The manager *who gets the highest sales* will receive a big bonus. (Commas not used because the information is essential to the sentence.)

Mr. Ames, the manager who had the highest sales in May, received a big bonus. [Commas needed because the manager (Mr. Ames) has been identified and the information is not essential to the sentence.]

The computer, which was purchased from the Elm Office Supply Company, will be installed on the network next week.

An upper-division economics course, such as Money and Banking, is required for a degree in business.

States, dates, days, names, titles of people, and **publications** should be set off with commas when they are <u>not</u> necessary to the sentence.

The branch manager is leaving for El Paso, Texas.

Mr. Will, from the Hudson Bank in Albany, has been named to the State Board of Examiners.

The sales meeting will be held on Monday, January 30.

Mr. Tumbleweek, manager of the Finance Department, said that sales have increased this year.

Professor Eddy's latest book, *Electronic Calculations,* was published by the Radom Company. *(Commas needed because the book title is not essential to the sentence since the book is identified as his latest.)*

James Mackay's book about William Wallace has made the top ten list. *(No commas needed because the information about William Wallace is essential to identify which of Mackay's books made the top ten.)*

GP 3.5 DIRECT ADDRESS

Use commas to set off names in a direct address.

Yes, Mr. Alida, your application for a charge account has been approved.

We realize, Jan, that your financial status has improved.

GP 3.6 CONSECUTIVE ADJECTIVES

Use a comma to separate two consecutive adjectives that modify the same noun. Hint: Only use commas if (1) the sentence is logical if the adjectives are reversed, and (2) the sentence is logical if the word *and* can be inserted between the adjectives.

She is a capable, diligent consultant. (Comma needed because "and" can be substituted for the comma.)

The old brick school building will become a museum. (No comma because it does not make sense when "brick" and "old" are reversed or "and" is inserted between old and brick.)

GP 3.7 SERIES

When three or more items are listed in a series and the last item is preceded by *and, or,* or *nor,* separate the items with a comma. Although a trend has started to omit the comma before the conjunction, it is still common practice to include a comma before the conjunction.

The president, the vice president, and the corporate secretary were present at the annual stockholders' meeting.

Typing reports, filing correspondence, and answering the telephone are the receptionist's duties.

GP 3.8 ADVERB "TOO"

If the adverb *too* (meaning also) comes anywhere in the sentence except at the end of the sentence, set it off with commas.

You, too, can qualify for the loan.

Do you agree, too, that she should sign the petition?

Susan doesn't think we should pursue the merger too. (No comma.)

Pitfall **Do not set off the word "too" when it is used to mean excessively.**	She thought she was too good to start at the beginning salary. Jon's review was too good for a new employee.

GP 3.9 DATES

When the year follows the month and day, set it off with a comma after the day and after the year. If only the month and year are given, do not use commas.

The June 1, 2001, deadline has come and gone.

The workshop was held on Thursday, March 13, 2001, which was one week after we received the software.

She would have a complete set of National Geographics for 100 years if she wasn't missing the October 1990 issue. (No comma needed because only month and year given.)

GP 3.10 PERSONAL NAMES

Jr., Sr., and Esq.

Do not use commas to set off Jr. or Sr. unless the person requests you to. Do not use a comma with a number that identifies seniority. The term "Esq." Is always set off with commas.

> We invited Thomas Albers Sr. to join the board.
>
> The case was heard by Louis Fierro III.
>
> The introduction to the text was written by John's attorney, Wesley James, Esq.

Academic Degrees and Professional Titles

Use a comma before and after an abbreviated academic degree or a professional title when an individual's entire name is given.

> Professor Sandy Fain, Ed.D., will teach the class.
> Jaunita Kress, CPA, has just been hired.
>
> The new preacher is Reverend Troy Peters, D.D.
> Jon Lovett, Ph.D., was the graduation speaker.

GP 3.11 OMITTED WORDS

Use a comma when the word *that* has been omitted causing a break in the sentence flow.

> The problem is, many of the employees don't have time to attend training.
>
> Chances are, the two companies will merge.

Use a comma to show that repetitive words have been left out of a sentence. (Hint: This usually occurs when semicolons separate clauses.)

> The Product Department received a 10 percent budget increase; the Advertising Department, a 5 percent budget increase; and the Accounting Department, a 7 percent budget increase.

Use a comma to separate parts of balancing expressions with missing words.

> Here today, gone tomorrow is an old motto.
> Garbage in, garbage out should be emphasized.

GP 3.12 REPEATED WORDS

When words are repeated, they should be separated with a comma.

> He was chairperson of the committee a very, very long time ago.

GP 3.13 QUOTATIONS (also see GP 6.5)

If a direct quotation is interrupted by expressions such as *he said, she replied,* and so forth, it is called a split quotation. A comma and quotation mark <u>precede</u> the interrupting expression and a comma follows it. The continued expression is <u>preceded</u> by a quotation mark.

> "If your firm agrees," the secretary stated, "I shall set the meeting for July 11."

When a quoted question begins a sentence, keep the question mark before the closing quotation mark and <u>do not</u> insert a comma.

"Will she be well enough to travel so soon after her surgery?" the tour director asked.

GP 3.14   WITH NUMBERS

Commas are used to set off whole numbers with five or more figures. It is optional to use the comma with four digits, but the trend is to omit the comma.

Do not include commas in page, policy, serial, model, or check numbers.

25,000	64,600,974	3500
Acct. No. 9750	Model 60932	Page 1000

GP 3.15   IN COMPANY NAMES

Unless you know that the company uses a comma in its name to separate Inc., Ltd., Corp., etc., do not use a comma.

Power PC Inc. Sunstate Corp.	Snapshots, Inc. (company uses a comma in letterhead)

GP 4 SEMICOLON

GP 4.1 INDEPENDENT CLAUSES WITHOUT A CONNECTIVE

Use a semicolon between independent clauses that are not joined by connecting words such as coordinating conjunctions (*and, but, or, for, yet, so,* or *nor*). Note: If the independent clauses are lengthy, treat them as two sentences.

Employees in two departments wanted to change to a four-day workweek; employees in the other four departments did not want to make this change.

GP 4.2 INDEPENDENT CLAUSES WITH INTERNAL PUNCTUATION

When one or both independent clauses in a compound sentence contain internal punctuation, use a semicolon before the coordinate conjunction.

We sold Lots 21, 23, and 27; and Lots 22, 24, 25, and 26 are being rented.

Unless we plan ahead for the convention, we will not be able to reserve the hotel and meeting rooms needed for the conference; but we can't plan too far ahead without Mr. Smith's approval.

GP 4.3 TRANSITIONAL EXPRESSIONS

(See GP 3.3C for rules about using commas with transitional expressions.)

Use a semicolon <u>preceding</u> transitional expressions that connect <u>two independent clauses</u> or that introduce a following element. If transitional expressions such as the following are used to connect independent clauses or complete a thought, a semicolon is required before the transitional expression and a comma after it.

accordingly	however	that is
besides	moreover	then
consequently	namely	therefore
for example	nevertheless	thus
furthermore	otherwise	yet
hence	so	

We did not receive the sales figures on time; *consequently*, we could not bid.

We were represented at the conference by three employees; *namely*, John Adams, Betty Pierce, and Harriet Kressen.

Mrs. Royal's students are expert transcriptionists; for example, all their work was mailable on the first try.

Words of one syllable require only a semicolon in front and no comma following the word.

We did not receive the sales figures on time; thus we could not bid.

Pitfall	Example:
Transitional expressions only require semicolons when they link two independent clauses in the absence of a coordinating conjunction.	The employees wanted to settle the strike, and consequently they did not care about back pay. (Comma is used instead of a semicolon because the coordinating conjunction *and* was used.)

GP 4.4 SERIES WITH INTERNAL PUNCTUATION

Use a semicolon to separate items in a series that already contains commas.

We found that Jerry Dean, production supervisor; Ron Wirth, communications consultant; and Alice Reese, advertising manager, formerly held government jobs.

GP 4.5 DEPENDENT CLAUSES IN A SERIES

Use semicolons between dependent clauses in a series if they are long or contain internal punctuation. (A dependent clause is a group of related words that contain a verb and a subject for that verb but doesn't express a complete thought.)

If you have little computer knowledge; if you don't know that a mouse and CPU are computer terms; if you have no idea of how to surf the net, then this course is for you.

103

GP 5   COLON

GP 5.1 FOLLOWING INDEPENDENT CLAUSE

Use a colon before words that complete the thought or add to the clarity of the sentence. The words before the colon should be an independent clause.

The supervisor emphasizes one quality: accuracy.

The following items were requisitioned: paper clips, letterhead, and mouse pads.

The clerk should requisition the following items: paper clips, letterhead, and mouse pads.

The company attempted to present a good image to the public in two ways: the property was beautifully landscaped and the parking lots were surrounded by white picket fences.

The manager forgot this important rule: authority and responsibility should be equal.

The enclosed brochure explains several key points: how to start investing, how much money you should be putting into a retirement fund, and how to research stocks.

Pitfall	Example:
When an introductory element ends with a verb or a preposition, do not use a colon.	The committee consists *of* Dr. Thomas and Ms. Sidel. The training materials *include* transparencies, answer keys, and notes. The purchasing officer *obtained* new steel desks, adjustable chairs, and modular file cabinets. (No colons should be used.)

GP 6 QUOTATION MARKS

GP 6.1 DIRECT QUOTATIONS

The most common usage of quotation marks is to enclose a direct quotation (the exact words of a writer or speaker). Words such as *said, remarked, stated,* and *replied* frequently indicate a direct quotation.

"Be sure to follow the guidelines," said Amy.

The new employee remarked, "I thought the company had better benefits."

Pitfall	Example:
Don't use quotation marks with indirect quotations. **Hint:** Indirect quotations usually begin with *that* or *whether.*	The department chairperson asked his replacement whether he knew the company training policy. The department chairperson said that he did know the policy.

GP 6.2 SLANG OR UNUSUAL WORDS

Enclose technical terms, business jargon, and other words that the reader may not know with quotation marks. Also enclose slang expressions and words given special emphasis. Words introduced by *marked, signed, labeled,* and *entitled* are enclosed with quotations.

The envelope was marked "Confidential."

"Booting" your computer should involve following a simple procedure.

The words "may" and "can" are often used incorrectly.

GP 6.3 REFERENCE SOURCES, POEMS, ARTICLES, RADIO AND TV PROGRAMS

Underline or italicize titles of <u>complete published works</u> (books, newspapers, plays, operas, poems, songs, magazines, pamphlets). Also underline or italicize titles of television or radio series. *The trend is to italicize these items and underline only if the document is not prepared using a computer.*

<u>Place quotation marks</u> around <u>parts</u> of published works (chapters, articles, sections, titles of essays, short poems, lectures, and feature columns in newspapers). Use quotation marks around titles of segments or programs that are part of a television or radio series.

> The title of Dr. Mallinson's text is *Contemporary Personnel.*
>
> The section in this text titled "Employees' Handbook" contains information on completing a W-2 Form.
>
> She sang "Amazing Grace" with strong feelings.
>
> During the "Did You Know" segment of the *Ricki Lake* show, I learned that she ran away from home.

GP 6.4 PARAGRAPHS

Do not use quotation marks around quoted paragraphs that are four or more lines. Instead single space the paragraphs and indent them a half inch from each side margin.

> The research conducted by Maslow was the beginning of understanding the hierarchy of needs. According to Winslow (1999):
>
> > Maslow's research has had a tremendous effect on how individuals progress to the self-actualization stage. This was the . . .

GP 6.5 PLACEMENT OF COMMAS AND PERIODS

Place commas and periods <u>inside</u> the end quotation mark.

> The Harry Potter books are described as "magical," "adventurous," "humorous," and "compelling."
>
> The letter was marked "confidential," but she read it.

Periods and commas also go <u>inside</u> the single quotation mark. If a direct quotation is interrupted by expressions such as *he said, she replied,* etc., a comma and quotation mark <u>precede</u> the interrupting expression and a comma follows it. The continued expression is <u>preceded</u> by a quotation mark.

Mr. Dabler said in his recent letter, "I plan to join the Army if I am not accepted in the McCosh Company's training program."

"We need the program immediately," wrote Effrim Gratehound, who is the systems manager at the Gallop Company.

Dr. McIntosh instructed, "Please route to me any items marked 'Confidential.' "

"If your firm agrees," the secretary wrote, "I shall schedule the meeting for July 11."

Quoted Questions Beginning a Sentence

When a quoted question begins a sentence, keep the question mark before the closing quotation mark and <u>do not</u> insert a comma.

"Will she be well enough to travel so soon after her surgery?" the tour director asked.

GP 6.6 PLACEMENT OF QUESTION MARKS AND EXCLAMATION POINTS

Place question marks and exclamation points inside the closing quotation mark when they apply to only the quoted material. Place question marks or exclamation points outside the closing quotation mark when they apply to the entire sentence.

Mrs. Jones asked, "When do I receive my free copy of The Wall Street Journal?" (Only the quotation is a direct question.)

Did Ms. Jones say in her letter, "I received my free copy of The Wall Street Journal"? (Question applies to the entire sentence.)

She cried, "The file drawer fell on my back!"

GP 6.7 PLACEMENT OF SEMICOLONS AND COLONS

The semicolon and colon are always placed outside the end quotation mark.

At the last board meeting, the chairperson stated, "I will issue new policy guidelines within a week"; we have yet to see these guidelines.

Insert these items into an envelope that is preprinted "For Office Use Only":   the letter, two copies of the cash flow statement, and the official audit statement.

GP 7   HYPHEN

GP 7.1 BETWEEN COMPOUND ADJECTIVES AND COMPOUND JOB FUNCTIONS

Use a hyphen to join compound adjectives before a noun they modify.

She is a well-known lecturer.

A $25,000-a-year salary for a beginning teacher is common.

Pitfall	Example:
Do not put a hyphen between an adverb ending in "ly" and the word that follows.	The highly qualified manager was new.

Use a hyphen to join dual job duties performed by one person.

She was hired to be the director-producer of the play.

Nancy served as the secretary-treasurer for two years.

GP 7.2 RE, SELF, CO, PRE

RE

Do not use a hyphen with words beginning with *re* unless they need to be distinguished from other words with the same spelling but with a different meaning. Hyphenate these words to facilitate reading and avoid confusion. Usually when the base word begins with the letter "e" no hyphen is needed.

No hyphen needed	Hyphen needed so that word is not confused with another word.
reevaluate	re-sign (resign)
redo	re-sort (resort)
remake	re-collect (recollect)
reassure	re-covered (recovered)
reeducate	re-creation (recreation)
reemphasize	re-press (repress)

SELF

Use a hyphen when *self* is used as a prefix.

self-addressed	self-evident
self-paced	self-worth
self-help	self-destruct

CO

Hyphens are either used or not used with the prefix *co*.

coauthor	co-payment
coworker	co-op
cochair	co-owner
codefendant	co-organizer
copilot	co-officiate
coordinator	co-edition
cooperation	co-officiate

PRE

In most instances, the hyphen is omitted when the prefix *pre* is used.

preeminent preemployment preempt preexisting	pre-engineered

GP 7.3 SERIES MODIFYING THE SAME NOUN

Use a hyphen after each word or figure in a series that modifies the same noun.

Employees in the mailroom sort first-, second-, and third-class mail.

GP 7.4 CONSECUTIVE NUMBERS AND TIME PASSAGE

Numbers

Use a hyphen when consecutive numbers are used. Do not use a hyphen if the word *between* or *from* is used.

Renovations to Rooms 1A-35A will begin on Thursday.

The class was assigned to read from pages 10 to 50.

During the week of April 15-22, we were on vacation.

Time

Use a hyphen when consecutive time periods are used. Do not use a hyphen with *between* or *from*.

The course schedule showed the following times for math: 1:30 p.m.-2:30 p.m., 4:00 p.m.-5:00 p.m., and 7:00 p.m.–8:00 p.m.

The meeting will take place between 2:30 p.m. and 4:45 p.m.

The store hours are from 9 a.m. to 5 p.m.

GP 8   APOSTROPHE

The apostrophe is used primarily to show omission (contractions) or possession (adjectives).

GP 8.1 CONTRACTIONS

Use an apostrophe to indicate where letters have been omitted in a contraction, words, or figures.

you're (you are)	It's (it is or it has)
Class of '97 (1997)	rock 'n' roll

Pitfall	Example:
	Whose jacket was left in the car? (Possessive pronoun)
Don't mistake a possessive pronoun for a contraction.	*Who's* the new manager? (Contraction for who is)
	Its branch offices are located throughout the world. (Possessive pronoun)
	It's too late for us to vote. (Contraction for it is)

GP 8.2 POSSESSIVES: WORDS NOT ENDING IN "S"

Add an apostrophe and "s" to form the possessive of most words <u>not</u> ending in "s."

employee's	businessmen's
YMCA's	association's

GP 8.3 POSSESSIVES: WORDS ENDING IN "S"

Add only an apostrophe to plural nouns ending in "s."
Hint: In order to determine if a plural word is possessive, answer the question: Can the word be made the object of the preposition "of"?

Three *years'* experience is required.
We finished the project three years ago.

The *manager's* salary did not increase.
The managers did not receive a salary increase.

The sales office is located in Des Moines.

GP 8.4 POSSESSIVES USED WITH GERUNDS

The word preceding a gerund must be in the possessive form. (A gerund is a verb form ending in *ing* that is used as a noun.)

His *taking* a vacation in July will leave the front office understaffed during the peak season.

The investigator identified Mr. Smith's writing.

Sally's *working* late makes him nervous because no one else is in the building.

GP 8.5 POSSESSIVE PROPER NAMES THAT END WITH THE SOUND OF S OR Z

Add an apostrophe and an "s" to proper names of only one syllable and add only an apostrophe to proper names with more than one syllable.

> Ms. *Tompkins'* working late is hard on her children. (Tompkins–more than one syllable.)
>
> Roger *Cornelius'* presentation was excellent. (Cornelius –more than one syllable.)
>
> Mr. *Shultz's* house is on the right. (Shultz–one syllable.)

GP 8.6 POSSESSIVE COMPOUND WORDS

Add an apostrophe and *s* to the final syllable of the word.

> Her daughter-in-law's wedding was beautiful.

GP 8.7 JOINT OWNERSHIP POSSESSIVE

Add an apostrophe or an apostrophe and *s* to the last name in the series.

> Meyer and Mallinson's book is in its fifth edition.

If there is no joint ownership, add an apostrophe or an apostrophe and an "s" to each name in the series.

> Meyer's and Mallinson's texts have sold well, and each text is on back order.

GP 8.8 PLURALS OF NUMBERS, LETTERS, SYMBOLS, AND ABBREVIATIONS

Numbers and Figures

Add an apostrophe and an "s" to form the plurals of most letters and figures.

> We recommended that a different font be used so the I's didn't resemble 1's.
>
> She got four B's and two A's on her report card.

Use only an *s* when pluralizing numbers expressed as figures.

> It was in the late '90s that the Internet became popular.
>
> In the 1800s Susan B. Anthony fought for women's rights.
>
> There were several size 10s still on the rack.

Abbreviations

Add only an *s* to form plurals of all capital abbreviations.

> HMOs are not popular with many people.
> Terry earned two Ph.D.s before he was 35.

GP 9 PARENTHESES

GP 9.1 ENUMERATED ITEMS

Enclose figures or letters that are used as enumerated items in a paragraph with parentheses.

> The new software upgrade features the following enhancements: (1) expanded templates, (2) bullet formats, and (3) drop cap style.

GP 9.2 FIGURES WRITTEN IN WORDS

Enclose figures with parentheses when they verify numbers that are written in words.

> She paid forty (40) dollars.
> She paid forty dollars ($40).

GP 9.3 PUNCTUATION

Place the ending punctuation mark before the closing parenthesis in a parenthetical sentence.

End of sentence punctuation follows the closing parenthesis.

> Frank now lives in Los Alamos (or is it Las *Alamos?*).
>
> We should allow new employees to attend an orientation workshop. (This should decrease problems with following company policy.)
>
> Which room will be available for the new sales associate (all rooms in the Sales Department are in full use)?

GP 10 CAPITALIZATION

GP 10.1 PROPER NOUNS (BUSINESS AND ORGANIZATIONS)

Proper nouns (words that identify specific persons, places, and things) are capitalized.

Dr. Mallinson is busy.

The *American Automobile Association* is holding its annual conference in Orlando.

GP 10.2 DEPARTMENTS, DIVISIONS, SECTIONS, COMMITTEES, AND BOARDS

Capitalize the titles of departments, divisions, sections, committees, boards, and other subdivisions of the <u>company where the individual is employed</u>. Do not capitalize the titles when they refer to another company or when they do not refer to a specific organization.

All expense items for the current fiscal year must be submitted to the Accounting Department by June 30. (within the company)

The accounting department of Rogers & Black will increase its budget. (outside the organization)

The Board of Directors will meet next Thursday and the Finance Committee will give a report. (within the company)

Jonathan Edwards has been elected to the board of directors of the Harrison Corporation. (outside the company)

GP 10.3   JOB TITLES

Capitalize a job or position title when it is used
preceding a name. Do not capitalize occupational titles
such as *author, surgeon, publisher,* and *lawyer.* Do not
capitalize job titles when they stand alone.

The meeting was called to order by President
Ross.

We were fortunate to have Councilman Stuart
support our position on the sales issue.

The plays of author Justin Allison won the most
awards.

Jane Allison was the author of the play.

The managing editor was promoted to senior
accountant before retiring.

Pitfall	Example:
Do not capital-ize titles when an apposition is used with a personal name except for the *President of the United States.*	The president, Bill Ross, called the meeting to order. Our Sales Department manager, Allison Page, won an award for being the top salesperson in her district. The President of the United States, George W. Bush, has gained support in the Midwest. Glenda Hood, mayor of Orlando, was reelected.

GP 10.4 PLACES: BUILDINGS, ROOMS, MOUNTAINS, RIVERS, MONUMENTS, AND STREETS

Capitalize the names of specific rooms and buildings. Also capitalize the names of places such as parks, monuments, rivers, oceans, and mountains.

The Parker Building is the newest addition to the downtown area.

The equipment will be set up in Exhibit Hall B.

The Sacramento River is beautiful.

The Mall of America in Minnesota is one of the largest in the world.

GP 10.5 TRADE NAMES

Capitalize trade names, product brands, and words that identify specific services offered by an organization.

Our new syrup, Connoisseur's Delight, is scheduled to be on the market by March 1.

Your Money Plus Account will be established as soon as we receive your application.

GP 10.6 DOCUMENTS AND LAWS

Capitalize titles of business forms, legal documents, and laws.

Please complete the Customer Survey Form and return it in the enclosed envelope.

The Articles of Incorporation were filed on July 1.

Make sure that any references to credit in the advertisement conform to the requirements of the Consumer Credit Protection Act.

GP 10.7 BOOKS, MAGAZINES, ARTICLES, AND SPEECHES

Capitalize each word in the title of a book, magazine, article, and speech with the exception of (1) articles (a, an, the) and (2) prepositions and conjunctions containing not more than three letters (e.g., for, of, or, but).

Ms. Hale's presentation is "Beyond Computing."

The bulletin *Energy Outlook* includes a section entitled "Ten Ways to Save Energy in the Office."

GP 10.8 COMPASS POINTS

Compass points are capitalized when they are used as adjectives to identify specific geographical areas of cities, states, countries, or the world. Some commonly recognized proper nouns and adjectives are:

- Cities: the South Side (Chicago), the East Side (New York).

- States: Southern California, West Texas.

- United States: the East, the West, the North, the South, the East Coast, the West Coast, the Midwest, the Southwest, the Pacific Northwest, the Eastern Seaboard.

- World: the Far East, the Middle East, Western Europe

The new department manager formerly worked at one of our branches in the East.

Sales in our Midwest branches have dropped since the hot weather began.

She lost her purse when she was out West.

Pitfall	Example:
Do not capitalize compass points that indicate direction when they come before the name of a place.	Heavy rain and hail have damaged much of the corn crop in eastern Nebraska and western Iowa.

GP 10.9   QUOTED SENTENCE

Capitalize the first word in a quoted sentence.

The new manager quoted from the employee handbook, "A doctor's notice is required for absences of more than two days."

GP 10.10   LETTERS AND NUMBERS

Capitalize the word before an identifying letter. Capitalize the word before an identifying number except when the word is *line, page, paragraph,* and *size.* If used, the word *Number* is usually abbreviated *No.* Generally, there is no need to use *No.* for identification.

Please check the prices on Invoice 64832.

The new regulations make the information in Bulletin No. 1 obsolete.

Only Table 7 was reserved.   (or)   Only Table No. 7 was reserved.

We did not process *Purchase Order 4321.*

The complete list of names was included in *Section G* of *Appendix C* on *page 19.*

GP 10.11 COURSE TITLES, SUBJECTS, AND ACADEMIC DEGREES

Only <u>specific</u> course titles should be capitalized. <u>General</u> names of subjects or areas of study should <u>not</u> be capitalized. Capitalize an academic degree only if it is used after a person's name.

She will receive her *bachelor of arts degree* when she takes the one required class left, *American Literature 9888.*

She hopes to get her *master of science degree* in *American literature.*

When he gets his degree, he will have his name printed in the research article in this format: *Howard Rodriquez, Doctor of Philosophy.*

GP 10.12 RACES AND LANGUAGES

Capitalize the formal name of races, languages, and heritages.

English, Spanish, Haitian, American, Oriental, Hispanic, Japanese, Caucasian, Afro American

(Note: black and white would not be capitalized, but Caucasian and Afro American are.)

GP 10.13 GOVERNMENT AGENCIES

Capitalize specific names of foreign, national, state, and local government units.

Traffic Commission
Office of Consumer Affairs
The Senate
United States Senate
British Empire
Florida's Child Welfare Agency

GP 11 DASH

GP 11.1 BEFORE SUMMARIZING WORDS

When the words *all, these,* and *they* are used as subjects that summarize preceding lists, use a dash in front of them. The dash is used <u>only when there is no verb used.</u>

The keyboard, computer, printer, modular desk furniture, and chair—all-important elements of a workstation—were ordered.

Internet access, global customer database, and good employees—these are the ingredients necessary to succeed in business today.

GP 11.2 DASH USED IN PLACE OF OTHER PUNCTUATION

Dashes can be used in place of commas, semicolons, colons, and parentheses. Generally dashes are used in place of other punctuation when more emphasis is desired.

In Place of Commas

Doing business on the Internet is often fast paced, productive, exciting, and—for me—tiring.

Of the numerous options offered the employees who lost their jobs in the merger, there was only one that most of them found acceptable—transferring.

All one hundred of the employees—including their supervisors—lost their jobs in the company's downsizing.

In Place of Semicolons

She paid the power bill—he paid the mortgage.

The report needs to be done—moreover, it needs to be done immediately.

In Place of Colons

Nancy is my friend as well as a colleague, and we share many things—namely, our love of fishing.

GP 11.3 DASH USED TO STRESS SINGLE WORDS

> The secret of less stress, however, is simple—rest!

GP 11.4 DASH USED WITH REPETITIONS AND RESTATEMENTS

> Suzie did as requested—finished the research for the report, typed the rough draft, made the revisions, and submitted the final copy to the manager who requested it—only to be told that Pete had already done the work.
>
> Don't let this great offer—a great offer too good to be true—go by.

GP 12 NUMBERS

(See GP 14 for rules concerning percents, decimals, and fractions. See GP 3.14 for rules about policies, and serial and model numbers.)

GP 12.1 ABOVE AND BELOW TEN

- Express numbers <u>through</u> ten in words unless they are used in tables, dates, amounts, or statistical text.

- Express numbers <u>above</u> ten in figures. In some formal situations, numbers above ten may be written as words. The general rule, however, is to use figures unless otherwise directed to do so or for more formal emphasis such as in the instance of "a hundred and one reasons."

- The current trend is to not use a comma in four digit numbers (1000) but to use commas in numbers of five digits or more (23,658).

The advertisement that was marketed toward the *40-plus* age group drew *120* requests.

We ordered *five* copies of the draft.

On *May 3* we wrote a *$5* check to cover the cost of the materials used by the *five-year-olds* in the class.

She received over 2000 entries.

GP 12.2 BELOW AND ABOVE 10 USED IN THE SAME SENTENCE

Express numbers used in a series in the same style. If one or more in the group is above ten, use figures for all numbers.

If the numbers are not in a series, express them both in words or figures.

The order was placed for *3* reams of paper, *15* cases of paper clips, and *10* toner cartridges.

Out of 55 students, *three* students got a score of *100* on their papers.

GP 12.3 BEGINNING OF A SENTENCE

Numbers at the beginning of a sentence are always spelled out. Spell out the word *number* at the beginning of a sentence instead of using the abbreviation No.

One hundred people attended the party.

Number 7654 was the original purchase order.

GP 12.4 DATES

Express dates in figures. Use endings (st, nd, rd, th) when the day precedes the month or is used alone.

She received her bill on *May 10*, which was her birthday.

The letter requested an RSVP by the *10th of May*.

GP 12.5 ORDINALS

Express ordinal numbers (example: first, fifteenth, twenty-second) in words. However, if the ordinals cannot be written in one or two words, express them in figures with one of these endings: st, nd, rd, th. A current trend is to replace "nd" and "rd" with "d."

According to the memo of May 5, her office was moved to the Finance Department on the *fifth* floor and decorated with *twentieth-century* art.

The company will celebrate its *twenty-fifth* anniversary with a big sale.

During this anniversary sale, the *150th* customer will receive a new car.

GP 12.6 MEASUREMENTS

Express the following measurements in figures:

Dimensions   Distances
Temperatures   Fluid measures
Weights   Electrical measures
Sizes

Her new office is *12* feet by *10* feet.

We have plenty of dresses in size *12*, but only three in size *6*.

The *30-pound* computer has been replaced with the *5-pound* laptop computer.

It cost the company $1,000 for *900 gallons* of gas.

GP 12.7 COMBINATIONS

When two numbers appear consecutively in a sentence and one is used as an adjective, express the first number in words and the second number in figures. However, if the second number is much shorter, express it in words and the first number in figures.

We ordered *six 25-pound* boxes of paper.

The original order called for *38 eight-page* brochures.

The new parking addition has added *two 150-space* parking lots.

GP 12.8   AGES

Express general ages in words. Use figures if ages:

- have contractual or statistical significance such as legally mandated ages for specific events

- are given immediately after a name or include months and days

---

The minimum age for full-time employment in the federal government is *21*. (contractual)

Mary Alexander joined the staff when she was only *twenty*. (general)

Sara Thompson, 33, is ten years younger than her husband. (age following name)

He had worked exactly *3 years 2 months and 6 days* before he was fired. (includes month and day. Note that no commas are used between years, months, and days)

Wanda is planning to retire in her fifties. (general)

GP 13   MONEY

GP 13.1   AMOUNTS OF $1 OR MORE

Express amounts of $1 or more in figures preceded by a dollar sign. Express even dollar amounts without a decimal point and zeros unless there are amounts with decimals in the same sentence. Although the trend is to not put a comma in four digit numbers, many people still think it looks awkward to not include the comma in monetary amounts. Whatever method you choose to use, be consistent and either put the comma in or leave it out in all four-digit dollar amounts.

When a sentence has four-digit and five-digit numbers, use a comma in the four-digit number.

The cost of the supplies for the transcription course was *$15.00*, and the book cost *$32.75*.

The tuition for the course was *$1,200*.

GP 13.2 AMOUNTS UNDER $1

Express amounts under $1 in figures followed by the word *cents*. When amounts under and over $1 appear in a series, write all amounts with dollar signs and decimal points for consistency.

Examples of amounts under $1:

The enclosed coupon entitles you to *25 cents* off your next purchase.

Because of increasing costs, the price of coffee in the employee lounge has been raised to *50 cents* per cup.

The city and state sales tax on items 1, 2, and 3 amounted to *$.85, $1.25,* and *$.75,* respectively.

GP 13.3 AMOUNTS OF A MILLION OR MORE

Even amounts of a million or more are expressed with a figure followed by the word *million, billion,* etc.

Since the hailstorm in July, *1 million* policyholders in your area have been reimbursed for more than *$2 million* in financial losses.

GP 14 PERCENTAGES, DECIMALS, AND FRACTIONS

GP 14.1 PERCENTAGES

Express the percent in figures and spell out the word *percent* except in technical or banking material.

> Our twenty-fifth anniversary sale will give customers a *25 percent* discount on certain items.
>
> The interest rate on her Visa card was 18.5%.

GP 14. 2 DECIMALS

Express decimals in figures.

> Our net profit has increased *3.5* percent over the same period last year.
>
> The unemployment rate rose *.09* percent last month, compared with *1.2* percent the previous month.

GP 14.3 FRACTIONS

Express fractions in words with a hyphen between the two parts unless the fractions are combined with whole numbers or cannot be written in one or two words.

> Only *one-half* of the new employees were eligible for vacation.
>
> Our sales force has increased *2 1/2* times during the last two years, and our profit has increased 5 percent. (2 1/2 = fraction combined with a whole number.)
>
> The lens aperture must be no larger than *195/200* of an inch. (Fraction cannot be written in one or two words.)

GP 15   TIME

GP 15.1   A.M., P.M., AND O'CLOCK

Express time in figures when the abbreviation a.m. or p.m. or the word o'clock follows the time. Use words to express time when it is not followed by a.m., p.m., or o'clock. Do not use zeros for time that is "on the hour."

Our plane leaves Denver at *11:30 a.m.* and arrives in Chicago at *2:40 p.m.*

The meeting will begin promptly at *2 p.m.* and will adjourn at *4:30 p.m.*

Professor Gifford's office hours are from *nine* to *eleven* Tuesday and Thursday.

We would like all conference participants to be our guests for lunch at *twelve-thirty.*

GP 15.2   PERIODS OF TIME (DAYS, MONTHS, YEARS)

Express periods of time in words except: (1) when the number cannot be expressed in one or two words, (2) when the time period is part of credit terms, discount periods, interest rates, or significant contractual terms.

Mr. Alderson has been president for *eight* years.

She has been employed for only *five months* and has already become the top salesperson in the district.

The company was founded *thirty-three* years ago.

The contract terms specify that the payment is due within *10 days* of receipt.

GP 16 ABBREVIATIONS

GP 16.1 TITLES

Do not abbreviate professional, military, and civil titles when used with surnames only. The abbreviation Dr. may be used, however, for Doctor.

> Professor Anderson introduced the speaker, Dr. Reed.

GP 16.2 ACADEMIC DEGREES

Abbreviate academic degrees and professional designations.

> Sheila Pham, *M.D.,* will become the new hospital director in early May.
>
> Professor Harold Smith, *Ph.D.,* will leave the faculty at the end of the school year to take a sabbatical. (Professor and Ph.D. do not mean the same; both titles can be used.)

GP 16.3 ORGANIZATIONS

The names of well-known organizations and agencies (business, government, military, professional, educational, and others) are frequently abbreviated.

Following are some common abbreviations. Notice they are typed in all capitals with no periods.

ORGANIZATIONAL ABBREVIATIONS

ABC	American Broadcasting System
ACLU	American Civil Liberties Union
AMA	American Medical Association
ARMA	Association of Records Managers and Administrators
ASTD	American Society of Training Directors
AT&T	American Telephone & Telegraph
CBS	Columbia Broadcasting System
EEOC	Equal Employment Opportunity Commission
EPA	Environmental Protection Agency
FAA	Federal Aviation Administration
FBI	Federal Bureau of Investigation
FCC	Federal Communications Commission
FDA	Food and Drug Administration
FDIC	Federal Deposit Insurance Corporation
FRS	Federal Reserve System
FTC	Federal Trade Commission
GM	General Motors
IBM	International Business Machines
IRS	Internal Revenue Service
NASA	National Aeronautics and Space Administration
NBC	National Broadcasting Company
NEA	National Education Association
OSHA	Occupational Safety and Health Administration
PBS	Public Broadcasting System
SBA	Small Business Administration
SCORE	Service Corps of Retired Executives
SEC	Securities and Exchange Commission
UCLA	University of California at Los Angeles
UPS	United Parcel Service
USAF	United States Air Force
USDA	United States Department of Agriculture
USPS	United States Postal Service

Representatives from the *IRS* will be available to answer questions.

We must follow the *EPA* guidelines in the handling of oil spills.

GP 16.4 BUSINESS NAMES

The words *Co., Corp., Inc.,* and *Ltd.* are frequently abbreviated in names of business organizations. *L.L.C.* is a new entity that has become popular. Follow the form indicated in the official name of the organization.

> *Edmond & Co.* was awarded the construction contract for the new municipal building.

GP 16.5 RADIO AND TV

Call letters of radio and television stations are written in capital letters without spaces or periods. TV, AM, and FM designations are usually separated from the call letters by a hyphen.

> Radio Station *WWXR-FM* will appeal the revocation of its license by the *FCC*.

GP 16.6 BUSINESS TERMS

Some business terms are expressed in lowercase letters separated by periods:

c.o.d., f.o.b., a.m., and *p.m.*

The following abbreviations are also expressed in lowercase letters but do not use periods:

ft, yd, bps, rpm, mpg, cpi, wpm, kg, km, and *mph.*

A few abbreviations use a mixture of capital and lower case letters

MHz, Corp., Mfg., Bros., Ltd., Inc., B.Ed. (Bachelor of Education), Ed.D. (Doctor of Education), Ph.D. (Doctor of Philosophy)

Other business terms are abbreviated and expressed in capital letters without periods. A few terms, such as academic degrees, use periods and all capitals. The following are some frequently used business abbreviations that are expressed in the all-capital format.

A.A.	Associate of Arts
ADA	Americans with Disabilities Act
AI	artificial intelligence
ARM	adjustable rate mortgage
APR	annual percentage rate
A.S.	Associate of Science
ASAP	as soon as possible
ATM	automatic teller machine
AV	audio visual
B.A.	Bachelor of Arts
BASIC	Beginner's All-Purpose Symbolic Instruction Code (programming language)
B.B.A	Bachelor of Business Administration
BBS	bulletin board system
BFOQ	bona fide occupational qualifications
B.S.	Bachelor of Science
CAD	computer-aided design
CAI	computer-assisted instruction
CAR	computer-assisted retrieval
CBT	computer-based training
CD	certificate of deposit
CD-ROM	Compact disc
CEO	chief executive officer
CFO	Chief financial officer
CFP	Certified financial planner
COBOL	Common Business Oriented Language (business programming language)
COLA	cost-of-living adjustment
CPA	certified public accountant
CPI	consumer price index

CPM	cost per thousand impressions
CPS	Certified Professional Secretary
CPU	central processing unit (of computer)
CRT	cathode-ray tube
CTS	carpal tunnel syndrome
DBMS	database management system (database software)
DPI	dots per inch
DRAM	dynamic random access memory
DSS	decision support system
DTP	desktop publishing
DVD	digital video disc
EAP	employee assistance program
EDT	Eastern
EEOC	Equal Employment Opportunity Commission
EFT	electronic funds transfer
EPS	encapsulated postscript
ERIC	Educational Resources Information Center
ESOP	employee stock ownership plan
EST	Eastern standard time
FAQ	frequently asked questions
FAX	facsimile
FIFO	first in, first out
FJA	functional job analysis
FLSA	Fair Labor Standards Act
FMLA	Family and Medical Leave Act of 1993
FOB	free on board-destination/shipping point
FTP	file transfer protocol
G or GB	gigabyte
GAAP	generally accepted accounting principles
GIF	graphics interchange format
GIGO	garbage in, garbage out
GPN	gross national product
GUI	graphical user interface
HMO	health maintenance organization
HTML	hypertext markup language
HTTP	hypertext transfer protocol
IRA	individual retirement account
ISP	Internet service provider
J.D.	Doctor of Jurisprudence
JPEG	joint photographic experts group
K	kilobyte
LAN	local area network

LCD	liquid crystal display
LCL	less than carload lot
L.H.D.	Doctor of Humanities
LIFO	last in, first out
M.A.	Master of Arts
M.B.A.	Master of Business Administration
MD	Medical Doctor
MIPS	millions of instructions per second
MIS	management information system
MPEG	moving picture experts group
NRC	noise-reduction coefficient
OCR	optical character recognition
OEM	original equipment manufacturer
OJT	on-the-job training
OLE	object linking and embedding
OS	operating system
PAQ	position analysis questionnaire
PC	personal computer
PDA	personal digital assistant
PDF	portable document format
PDT	Pacific daylight time
PERT	Program Evaluation and Review Technique
PPO	preferred provider organization
PPP	point-to-point protocol
PR	public relations
PST	Pacific standard time
RAM	random access memory
RN	Registered Nurse
ROM	read-only memory
R&D R/D	research and development
RPG	report program generator (program language)
RSI	repetitive strain injury
S&L	savings and loan association
SCSI	small system computer interface
SLIP	Serial line Internet protocol
SOHO	acronym for "small office/home office
STMD	supervisory training and management development
TCP/IP	transmission control protocol/Internet protocol
TIFF	tagged image file format
TQM	total quality management

TRA	Tax Reform Act
UPS	uninterruptible power supply;
	United Parcel Service
URL	uniform resource locator
USB	universal serial bus
VDT	video display terminal
VM	voice mail
WAN	wide-area network
WATS	wide-area telecommunications service
www	world wide web
WYSIWYG	what you see is what you get
ZIP	compressed files disk
	zone improvement plan

Sally had no experience when she began doing *PR* work for the company.

Since your past-due account has not been paid, we must ship your July 1 order c.o.d.

GP 17   SUBJECT/PRONOUN AND VERB AGREEMENT

GP 17.1   EACH, EVERY, ANY, MANY A, MANY AN

When *each, every, any, many a*, and *many an*, are used as adjectives, the subjects that are modified require a singular verb. This rule also applies when the sentence has more than one subject.

<u>Every</u> transcription operator and word processing secretary <u>needs</u> to learn Microsoft Word.

<u>Many an</u> employee and manager <u>has</u> received overtime.

<u>Each</u> new student and his or her teacher <u>has</u> an orientation packet.

GP 17.2   EITHER/OR AND NEITHER/NOR

Whether or not the verb is singular or plural in sentences with compound subjects joined by "or" or "nor" is determined by the subject closest to the verb.

Either the word processing operators or their **supervisor is** going to transcribe Mr. Smith's work.

Neither the supervisor nor the word processing **operators are** going to transcribe Mr. Smith's work.

GP 17.3   SUBJECT/PHRASE

The subject is <u>not</u> part of a phrase; therefore, disregard phrases in determining the subject. Exclude prepositional phrases and phrases beginning with *in addition to, as well as, together with, in conjunction with, etc.*, when determining the subject. The verb used should agree with the subject.

One of the students **is** absent.

The **instructor**, as well as the students, **has** trouble reading the print in the book.

The awards **ceremony**, in conjunction with the retirement party, **is** scheduled for May 10.

GP 17.4   INVERTED SENTENCES

When sentences are inverted, the subject comes after the verb.

In addition to the new policies **is** a regulation **handbook** available to all employees.

Have the new policy **handbooks** been given to all employees?

GP 17.5 INDEFINITE PRONOUNS

GP 17.5A SINGULAR INDEFINITE PRONOUNS

These indefinite pronouns always require a singular verb. This rule also applies when there are two subjects in sentences joined by "and."

another	either	neither
any	every	no one
anybody	everybody	nobody
anyone	everyone	nothing
anything	everything	somebody
each	more	someone
each one	much	something

Someone in the class **travels** 100 miles a day.

Every member of the swim team **practices** swimming techniques daily.

Every machine transcription operator <u>and</u> division supervisor **has** been given a copy of the reference manual.

GP 17.5B PLURAL INDEFINITE PRONOUNS BOTH, FEW, MANY, OTHERS, AND SEVERAL

A plural verb is needed with *both, few, many, others,* and *several.*

Several of the new employees **are** in training classes.

Both of the computers **need** more memory.

GP 17.5C INDEFINITE PRONOUNS SOME, ANY, MORE, MOST, ALL, NONE

Indefinite pronouns *some, most, none,* and *all* take either singular or plural verbs. If these words tell how much, the verb is singular. If these words tell how many, the verb is plural. The verb depends on whether the pronoun refers to something singular or plural.

> **All** of the students **have** their homework finished. (how many—refers to students)
>
> **All** of the land purchased in 1995 **has** been built on. (how much—refers to land)
>
> **Most** of the new policy handbooks **have** been given to all employees. (how many—refers to handbooks)
>
> **Some** of the committee members **were** not present when the vote was made. (how many—refers to members)

GP 17.6 THE PRONOUN "YOU"

The pronoun "you" requires a <u>plural</u> verb.

> You are not going to pass the test if you don't study.

GP 17.7 COLLECTIVE NOUNS

Collective nouns usually take singular verbs; however, members of a group acting individually take plural verbs.

> The Ad Hoc **Committee meets** this afternoon. (Committee acting as one group)
>
> The Ad Hoc **Committee** comprised of individuals from several different ethnic groups **are** discussing the development of the cultural awareness curriculum. (Committee with members acting individually)

144

GP 17.8 NOUNS ENDING IN "ICS"

When a noun ending in "ics" refers to one topic or body, use a singular verb. When it refers to a plural meaning, use a plural verb.

Statistics was the hardest course he took in college.

The 2000 census statistics are now being analyzed.

Mathematics is a subject that may people dislike.

The mathematics on the state exam cover business math, algebra, geometry, and calculus.

The acoustics in the theater are terrible.

The physics needed for the experiment is very complex.

GP 17.9 NOUNS ENDING IN "S" THAT ARE NOT PLURAL

Although some words end in "s" they are not plural. Examples of these words include news, summons, measles, and lens.

The **news** covers timely community happenings.

Measles is a disease that now has a preventive shot.

The **summons is** supposed to be delivered on Monday. (Plural would be summonses.)

The **lens** on the camera needs to be replaced. (Plural would be lenses.)

GP 17.10 NOUNS ENDING IN "S" THAT ARE PLURAL

Some nouns ending in "s" refer to one item, but they require plural verbs. Examples of these words are:

credentials	odds	proceeds	premises
earnings	dyes	savings	assets

> The odds of his winning are small.
> His earnings are about to increase with his new territory.

GP 17.11 NOUNS ENDING IN "S" THAT ARE PLURAL UNLESS PRECEDED BY "PAIR OF"

Certain words such as *scissors, pliers, glasses, pants,* and *trousers* are plural unless "pair of" is in front.

> The scissors are in the drawer.
> The pair of scissors in the drawer needs to be sharpened.

GP 17.12 FRACTIONS AND PORTIONAL AMOUNTS

Fractions or portions such as *half, one-fourth, none, part of, majority of,* and *a portion of* take singular or plural verbs according to the modified noun. Hint: If the word following "of" is plural, use a plural verb. If it is singular, use a singular verb.

> **One-fourth** of the machine transcription **operators are** scheduled to work the third shift.
>
> A large **portion of** the **meat** in the freezer **is** spoiled.
>
> Insufficient training **is part of** the **problem** causing new employees to code the projects incorrectly.

GP 17.13   THE WORD "NUMBER"

Use a plural verb when "number" is preceded by "a." Use a singular verb when "number" is preceded by "the."

A **number** of employees **are** receiving raises.

The number of employees receiving raises **is** increasing.

GP 18   PRONOUN/ANTECEDENT AGREEMENT

GP 18.1   AGREEMENT IN NUMBER

A pronoun must agree in number (singular or plural) with its antecedent (the noun to which the pronoun refers).

Every **student** should come to class prepared with **his** or **her** pencil, text, and paper.

All of the **students** have **their** books.

GP 18.2   AGREEMENT IN PERSON

Pronouns must agree in person (first–person(s) speaking; second–person(s) spoken to; third–person(s) spoken about). A common agreement problem in person is to use "you" with a third-person antecedent.

Correct:
When the transcription **operators** have trouble understanding the dictation, **they** should request clarification from the dictator.

Incorrect:
When the transcription **operators** have trouble understanding the dictation, **you** should request clarification from the dictator.

GP 18.3 AGREEMENT WITH "OR" OR "NOR"

If the antecedents joined by "or" or "nor" are singular, use a singular pronoun. If the antecedents are plural, use a plural pronoun.

If the antecedents are plural and singular, the antecedent closest to "nor" or "or" is used to determine if a singular or plural pronoun is used.

Matosha Travick-McGill or Adelma Strickland will receive **her** award at the ceremony.

The two new transcription operators or the three new secretaries will receive **their** orientation on Monday.

Neither the assistant director nor the employees were happy about **their** pay.

Neither the employees nor the assistant director was happy about **his** pay.

GP 19 VERB TENSE AGREEMENT

GP 19.1 PRESENT TENSE

The present tense of a verb is usually designated by a main verb and agrees with the subject. Sometimes, an "s" is added to the end of the verb.

The supervisor **listens** to all dictation first.

The transcription operators **check** their work.

GP 19.2   PAST TENSE

Adding "d" or "ed" to the present tense of the verb usually shows past tense.

> The transcription operators **checked** their work.

GP 19.3   FUTURE TENSE

The future tense of a verb is used when the action will take place in the future. Future tense is shown by adding the helping verbs "shall" or "will" to the main verb.

Use "shall" with first person (I).
Use "will" with the third person (he, she, it) or other nouns.

The trend is to use "shall" only in formal situations and "will" in everyday usage.

> The transcription **operators will check** their work.
>
> **I shall check** my transcription before initializing it.

GP 19.4   PRESENT PERFECT TENSE

Using "has" or "have" and the past tense of the verb forms present perfect tense.

> The transcription **operators have checked** their work.
>
> The sales **director has reviewed** the final report.

GP 19.5   PAST PERFECT TENSE

Using "had" with the past tense of the verb or its participle forms past perfect tense.

The transcription **operators had checked** their work and were given permission to leave early.

GP 19.6   FUTURE PERFECT TENSE

Future perfect tense is formed by using "will" or "shall" with the present perfect tense (has or have).

The transcription **operators will have checked** their work before the end of the day when it is logged.

I shall have earned enough vacation time to take two weeks off this summer.

DOCUMENT FORMATS

DF 1 OVERVIEW OF LETTER STYLES

Most word processing software programs have templates that automatically format letters in a variety of styles. Unless the word processing software program is a version for business, it will not include professional letter templates. Instead it will have more "trendy" template styles that do not conform to business standards.

All letters <u>except</u> simplified should include the following:

- **return address** (address of the company or writer). If company letterhead is used, there is no need to type a return address in the letter.

- **date** (month, day, year)

- **inside address** (the name and address of the person the letter is being sent to)

- **salutation** ("Dear" followed by the title and last name of the person to whom the letter is being sent)

- **closing** (a word to signify the closing of the letter such as "Sincerely" or "Cordially")

- **originator's typed name** (the originator is the person who dictated, wrote, or drafted the letter)

- **reference initials** *only if the person typing the letter is <u>not</u> the one originating it.* Reference initials are the initials of the person who typed the letter but didn't originate it. They are typed in lower case a double space below the originator's typed name.

There are four primary letter styles:

- Block
- Modified-Block
- Modified-Block with Indented Paragraphs
- Simplified

The following chart shows the features of each letter style.

LETTER STYLES

STYLE	FEATURES
Block	All lines begin at left margin including date, closing, and reference initials.
Modified-Block	The body of the letter is blocked (all lines beginning at left margin); however, the date, complimentary closing, and originator's typed name begin at the center point.
Modified-Block with Indented Paragraphs	Format is the same as for modified-block except that the first line of each paragraph is indented five spaces.
Simplified Note: It is now becoming acceptable to not use all capitals for the typed originator's name.	All lines begin at the left margin. There is no salutation or complimentary close. There is an all-capital subject line typed on the second line below the inside address. The word "subject" is not typed to introduce it. Four returns are used after the body of the letter and then the name of the originator (writer) is typed in all capitals.

DOCUMENT SPACING

Document	Spacing
Letters Note: The simplified style does not have a salutation or a complimentary close.	Single space paragraphs and double space between them. Double space between the last line of the inside address and the salutation. Double space after the salutation and the beginning of the letter. Double space between the last paragraph and the closing. Double space twice (4 returns) after the closing before typing the writer's name. Double space after the writer's name and reference initials. Single space reference initials, enclosure, and copy notations unless there is room to double space them.
Memorandums	Double space between the heading information. Single space the body of the memo.
Reports	Double space the body of a report. Triple space after the title of the report. Double space before and after side headings.

155

DF 2 TWO-PAGE LETTERS

Use the following guides for typing a two-page letter:

1. A paragraph of four lines or more may be divided if at least two lines are placed on each page. Never place only the complimentary close and signature line on the second page.

2. Leave a bottom margin of at least 1 inch on the first page.

3. Type the name of the person the letter is addressed to, the page number, and the date at the top of the second page, starting 1 inch from the top of the page. Two common arrangements of this heading information follow.

    Use style (a) with a modified block style letter.
    Use style (b) with a block style letter.

    (a)
    Mr. Harvey Tolson   Page 2   March 9, 2002

    (b)
    Mr. Harvey Tolson
    Page 2
    March 9, 2002

    It is a good idea to type the heading for a two-page letter as a header in case the page break changes during editing.

4. Triple space between the second page heading and the body of the letter.

DF 3 INSIDE ADDRESS

An address may include any or all of the following items:

* addressee's name;
* addressee's job title;
* name of department or company division;
* company name;
* street address or post office box number;
* city, state, and ZIP Code. Always use the five-digit ZIP Code; the nine-digit ZIP Code is optional and used by companies with mass mailings.

The U.S. Postal Service wants addresses typed in all capitals without punctuation.

```
MR CHARLES FENNER
AMERICAN TECHNICAL ASSOCIATION
960 ANDERSON ST
OAKTON MD  23445-6789
```

Unless a mailing list is used, the most frequent method used to address an envelope for a letter is through word processing software. Word processing software will print the inside address from a letter on an envelope. The address is printed exactly as it was keyed in the letter, therefore, unless the address was keyed in the U.S. Postal style of all capitals and no punctuation, the address will be in traditional style.

It looks awkward to have an all capital, no punctuation address in the letter when the rest of the letter is in lower case. However, this inside address style may become acceptable in the mainstream as technology drives format changes. Until then, using the "Change Case" format feature in word processing software programs makes it easy to change traditional envelope formatting to the preferred U.S. Postal Service style.

The mail merge feature in word processing software can be used to change to the "all caps, no punctuation" style.

Address Format

See GR 7 Address Rules and Guidelines, Section Inside and Envelope Address Guidelines, for specific information on how to handle department names, post office numbers, etc.

See GR 8 for information on the two-letter state abbreviations.

See GR 11 for information on how to address international mail.

Type each part of the address on a separate line, except for single-word titles, which may follow the person's name on the same line.

DF 4   ATTENTION LINE

See Figure 3.

An attention line is used for the following purposes:

1. When you only know the title or position and not an individual's name.

2. When you know the individual's name but want to make it clear that if that person leaves the company, anyone in the company may open the correspondence.

Since letters that are of a personal or confidential nature are marked with these notations, it is considered acceptable to open correspondence addressed to an individual no longer employed at a company. *Attention lines, therefore, are usually not necessary and using them should be avoided.*

Envelope Address

On the envelope the attention line should be typed as the first line of the address.

ATTN: MR. PAUL ANDERSON
MARINE ENTERPRISES INC
1087 MAIN ST
RICHMOND VA 22042-1441

or

ATTN: SALES DEPARTMENT MANAGER
MARINE ENTERPRISES INC
1087 MAIN ST
RICHMOND VA 22042-1441

Letter

- Since the attention line is included as the first line of the address as shown above, it is not necessary to include an attention line in the letter.

- An "organizational" salutation such as "Ladies and Gentlemen" should be used or the salutation should include the name of the department in the attention line.

- Type the salutation a double space below the inside address. (Note that the salutation is directed to the company, not the individual as shown below.)

Attention: Mr. Fred Parsons
Indiana Electronic Components
57873 Industrial Park Road
Gary, IN 46401

Ladies and Gentlemen:

```
Attention:  Marketing Manager
Indiana Electronic Components
57873 Industrial Park Road
Gary, IN  46401

Dear Sir or Madam:
```

DF 5 SALUTATION

The most common salutation is Dear. If the writer and letter recipient have a close relationship, the recipient's first name may be used in the salutation. If the relationship is more formal, the recipient's title and last name should be used. A colon is usually used in the salutation unless the letter style uses open punctuation.

Item	(Salutation)
Addressee's title and gender are known	Use title given. If no title is given for a woman, use Ms. *Dear Ms. Whitehead*
Addressee's gender is unknown because initials are used or name doesn't denote gender.	Do not use any courtesy title in address or salutation. Use the addressee's first and last name. *Leslie Anderson* *Dear Leslie Anderson:*
Addressees are husband and wife sharing same last name.	Traditional: Use Mr. and Mrs. (do not use "&" for "and"). *Dear Mr. and Mrs. Ferguson*
Attention Line	Use one of the formats shown in DF 4.

Item	(Salutation)
Organizations with both men and women	Do not use Gentlemen. Use "Ladies and Gentlemen" in the salutation.
Unmarried Individuals	If the names are short enough, put them both on the first line. If they are too long to do so, put them on separate lines. *Ms. Pat Daniels and Mr. Chris Johns* 2298 Oakridge Street New York, NY 10128 or *Ms. Cassandra Strickland* *Ms. Carolyn Vandergrift* 2298 Oakridge Street New York, NY 10128 If the correspondence is informal, use only first names in the salutation. If the correspondence is formal or business related, use titles with last names in the salutation. *Dear Pat and Chris:* *Dear Ms. Daniels and Mr. Johns:*

The chart below shows sample address and salutations for professionals and officials:

Individual	Inside Address	Salutation
Attorney	Ms. Sara Sanders Attorney–at–Law or Sara Sanders, Esq.	Dear Ms. Sanders
Dean of College	Dr. Paul Smith Dean of Education or Dean Paul Smith Education Dept.	Dear Dean Smith or Dear Dr. Smith
Episcopal Bishop	The Right Reverend Michael Denver	Dear Bishop Denver
First Lieutenant	First Lieutenant, Eugene Bahadori	Dear Lieutenant Bahadori
Governor	The Honorable Sara Nelson	Dear Governor Nelson
Judge	The Honorable Aramis Rodriquez	Dear Judge Rodriquez
Lieutenant Colonel	Lieutenant Colonel, Arthur Brown	Dear Colonel Brown
Mayor	The Honorable Angel Valenson	Dear Mayor Valenson
Nun	Sister Mary Dunlap	Dear Sister Dunlap
Priest	The Reverend Father Jon Fiorelli	Dear Father Fiorelli
Protestant Clergy	The Reverend Howatt Dixon	Dear Dr. Dixon
Rabbi	Rabbi John Bard	Dear Rabbi Bard
Representative	The Honorable Tony Encinias	Dear Representative Encinias
Senator	The Honorable Kelly Ferranti-DuBois	Dear Senator Ferranti-DuBois

DF 6   SUBJECT LINE

A subject or reference line identifies the content of the letter or calls attention to a specific file.

1. Type the subject line in all-capital letters or initial capitals a double space below the salutation. Double space between the subject line and the letter body.

Dear Paul:

Subject: Time Reports

The time reports from your district need to be turned in to the main office.

---

2. Begin the subject line at the left margin in a block style letter. In a modified block style letter with indented paragraphs, the subject line may be indented. The subject line may also be centered for special emphasis.

3. The word *Subject:* or *In RE, In re:* or *Re:* is usually typed before the subject line information except in a simplified letter. *Subject* is the more common subject format used.

SUBJECT: SPECIAL SALE

Subject: Special Sale

In re: Receptionist Vacancy

Refer to: Policy 160-7543

Re: Property of E. A. Black
         3094 South Ponderosa Avenue
         Denver, CO 80200

DF 7   PERSONAL OR CONFIDENTIAL NOTATIONS

Type a personal or confidential notation on the second line below the date at the left margin. The notation should be typed in all-capital letters in bold print.

June 23, 20–

CONFIDENTIAL

Dr. Gail Anderson
Parkway Medical Center
786 Houston Street
Maryville, TN 98409

Dear Dr. Anderson:

DF 8   POSTSCRIPT NOTATIONS

Postscripts are used for emphasis or to add information that was thought of after the letter was composed.

- If the letter contains indented paragraphs, indent the first line of the postscript; otherwise type it at the left margin.

- Type the postscript on the second line below the closing or the copy and enclosure notations if they are used.

- Type *PS:*   followed by two spaces and the beginning of the postscript. Occasionally writers leave off the *PS* initials, but this trend has not become common practice.

POSTSCRIPT PLACEMENT

We will ship the supplies immediately. Thank you for your understanding and patience.

Sincerely,

Jon Peterson, Marketing Director

mk

c Paul Johnson, Shipping Supervisor

PS: In the future we will have these items in stock so you should receive your orders within a few days from the time we receive your order.

DF 9   LISTS, ENUMERATIONS, QUOTATIONS

The body of a letter or report may include lists, enumerations, or quotations. A quick way to bullet or number items is to:

1. Type the items single spaced at the left margin followed by a return at the end of each item.

2. Highlight the items to be numbered or bulleted.

3. Click on the bullets or numbering icon on the formatting toolbar.

1. Indent **lists** five spaces or more from the left margin, capitalizing the first word of each item. Bullets or numbers may also be used.

> Business letters frequently include the following:
>
> - Attention line
> - Subject line
> - Enclosure notation
> - Copy notation

2. Follow any specific instructions for formatting **enumerations**, using the following examples as guides:

Example 1:

> These requirements will be satisfied if any of the following authorities are notified immediately: (1) the commanding officer of Coast Guard Unit 4, (2) the commander of the Texas Coast Guard District, or (3) the regional director of the EPA.

Example 2:

> The sale of your property can be handled in several ways:
>
> 1. Direct sale for cash
> 2. Direct sale for part cash; you can carry the mortgage
> 3. Company purchase of your property for immediate cash; we resell at our convenience

Example 3:

This letter is to confirm our telephone discussion in which we agreed that you would arrange for or perform the following work at these fields:

1. Change the crankcase oil in the Acme engine and the gearbox oil in the pumping unit; grease the pumping unit as necessary.

2. Purchase a sufficient number of fire extinguishers to meet the federal safety standards.

---

3. Align **subdivisions of enumerations** under the first word of the enumeration to which they refer as shown below.

Therefore, will you please contribute this input to the program with your next monthly report:

1. Ask 100 customers to complete the enclosed Survey Form

2. Evaluate the contribution of the department based on:

    a) the relationship to sales in other non-food departments.

    b) demographic characteristics of the population in the geographic area served by your store.

---

4. Indent and single-space **quotations consisting of four or more lines** five spaces from the left and right margins. Quotation marks are omitted.

> The current student handbook stresses the importance of attendance. As stated on page 13:
>
> > Because of the compressed, intensive nature of the graduate classes, students must attend all class sessions and adhere to the scheduled class hours.
> >
> > Absences will be excused only in cases of illness of the student or a death in the immediate family.

DF 10 CLOSING, REFERENCE, AND COPY NOTATIONS

Refer to Figure 3 for an example of how these closing, reference, and copy notations appear in a letter.

Closing

In addition to the complimentary closing and the originator's (writer's) typed name, the closing lines must include reference initials (if the person typing the letter is not the one originating it) and enclosure and copy notations when applicable. Some letters may also have postscripts.

1. The complimentary closing is typed a double space below the body. Common closings include Cordially, Cordially yours, Sincerely yours, Sincerely, Yours truly, and Respectfully (used when writing to judges and public figures).

2. The <u>originator's (writer's) name and title</u> are typed on the fourth line below the closing or the company name. If the title is long, it may be placed on a separate line below the typed name.

3. <u>Reference Initials</u>: If the writer did not type the letter, the initials of the person who typed the letter are typed in lower case a double space below the typed name of the writer.

Sincerely yours, (4 returns)

Jonathan Brown, Sales Director

lm

---

4. Enclosure or attachment notations are typed on the line below or a double space below the reference initials if there is room. When correspondence includes more than one enclosure or attachment, make sure the number is clear to the reader.

Enclosures (2)	Enclosures:
	    Check
	    Invoice

Attachment	Enc.

---

5. The copy notation is typed on the line below, or if there is room, a double space below the reference initials or enclosure notation, whichever is last. A variety of formats may be used. Although the "cc" notation is still used, a single "c" without a colon is becoming the preferred style.

A blind copy notation (bc) is used when the writer does not want the recipient of the letter to know that someone else will also receive a copy of the letter. The bc notation is typed a double space below the copy notation <u>on the copy only</u>. If there is no copy notation, type the bc notation a double space below the enclosure notation or reference initials.

169

The text following the copy notation should be 0.5 inches from the left margin.

c	Ms. Alice Parker (preferred style)
cc	R. Y. Beaumark
	Personnel Services
bc:	Tom Broers (typed on copies only)
cc	Arapahoe Corporation
	475 Nevada Street
	Denver, CO 8023
cc	R. Adams
	D. Long

DF 11   COMPANY   NAME   USED   IN CLOSING

Occasionally a letterhead may only have a logo and no distinguishable company name, or the writer may want to emphasize that the letter is being sent on behalf of the company. In these instances, the company name may be used in the closing. When the company name is used in the closing, it should be typed according to the following guidelines:

• Align the company name with the closing.

• Type the company name in all-capital letters on the second line below the closing.

Cordially yours,

METRO WEST WHOLESALERS

Samatha Jones, Vice President

DF 12   MEMORANDUMS

Refer to Figure 5 and Figure 6 for examples of memorandums.

Messages sent between offices within an organization are called memos, memorandums, or interoffice communications. Many companies use printed forms. Although the style of the forms may vary, the standard heading contains the following items: TO, FROM, DATE, and SUBJECT.

Many word processing software programs have a memo template that simplifies the formatting of memos. However, these templates do not follow standard business memo formats.   For instance, the copy notation is included in the heading information instead of at the bottom, which is standard memo format.

Follow these basic guidelines for typing memos:

Type the heading information:

On a printed form:

Align the text two spaces after the colon in the longest line of the heading.

On plain paper:

1. A heading such as Memorandum can be typed at the left or centered 2 inches from the top of the page. (If the memo is long, a 1-inch top margin can be used to avoid a second page.)

2. Clear tab settings and set a tab stop 10 spaces from the left margin.

3. Double space and type the headings (TO, FROM, DATE, SUBJECT). Tab after each heading item and type the text that corresponds to it. This should align the text two spaces after the colon in each heading entry.

- If the heading Memorandum is not included, then *MEMO TO:* should be used instead of *TO.*

- It is not necessary to use individual's titles (Mr., Ms., etc.). It may be helpful to include information such as a telephone extension or department name or title after FROM.

- If the memo is going to more than one person, try to fit all names on the same line. If there are too many names to fit on one line, either the names can be listed next to TO: or a distribution list can be included at the end of the memo.

- The word Distribution is typed underlined a triple space below the reference initials.

- Highlight or place a check in front of each name to indicate who is to receive that copy of the memo.

TO: Carl Lester, Leah Fairchild-Johnson

MEMO TO: J. A. Fast, Advertising
            Fred Beaumark, Publications
            Sarah Anderson, Accounting

Distribution:

C. Anderson
F. Beaumark
S. Anderson

- Some templates in word processing software include CC (copies) in the heading information. This is not standard formatting. If a copy will be sent to others, put the copy notation at the bottom of the memo.

- If the memo is confidential, type the word CONFIDENTIAL in all-capitals in boldface centered on the third line below the heading. Begin typing the body of the memo on the third line below the confidential notation.

4. Triple or double space after the last line of the heading.

5. Single-space the body. Use a 1-inch margin so that the text is flush with the printed headings.

6. If the originator of the memo requests, type in all capital letters his or her initials two lines after the last line of text in the body of the memo.

   The preferred trend is to type only the typist's initials a double space after the last line of text in the body of the memo.

7. If necessary, type a heading on the second page of a two-page memo using the same information and format used for a letter.

8. If reference initials (typist's initials) are needed, type them a double space below the last line of the body.

9. If necessary, type the appropriate enclosure (or attachment) and, if not included in the heading, type copy notations below the reference initials.

DF 13   PRESS AND NEWS RELEASE

Refer to Figure 7 for an illustration of a press release. A press or news release contains information that is sent to a newspaper, television station, or radio station in advance for publication or broadcast. All press releases must have heading lines that include the date, name of person to contact for more information, a phone number, and the words "For Immediate Release" or "For Release on ___."

Many word processing programs have templates to automatically format a news release. If a template is not available:

Format:

- Use 1 inch margins
- Single space the heading lines.
- Triple space after the heading.
- Double space or single space the body.
- Number all pages except the first.

Content Sections:

Release Statement: At the upper-left margin, in all capitals, key "FOR IMMEDIATE RELEASE" or "FOR RELEASE ON (key date)"

Contact Information: This should include the name, phone number(s), fax, and Email address of a person to contact for more information.

Headline: Should be one sentence and keyed in all capitals and bold.

Issued/Date Line: This information is keyed as the first part of the body of the release. It includes the city and state where the release is from and the date. Example: Orlando, FL, March 13, 20–.

174

<u>Additional Pages</u>: Key "more" centered at the bottom if the release is more than one page.

<u>End</u>: Type the three symbols *# # #* or *End* a double space below the end of the message to signify the end of the press release.

DF 14 AGENDA

Refer to Figure 8 for an illustration of an Agenda.

1. Type the word AGENDA in all capitals, centered and in bold type 2 inches from the top of the page.

2. Include information about the name, date, and location of the meeting in a heading, single spaced and typed a double space below the word AGENDA. You may also double space the heading material.

3. Use numbers to indicate items to be discussed in order during the meeting. Single space each item and double space between items.

DF 15 MINUTES

Refer to Figure 9 for an example of Minutes.

Minutes are written summaries of what was discussed and decided upon at a meeting.

There are a variety of different styles to use in formatting minutes. One style is to use paragraph form to report what action was taken. Another style is to use side headings so that the reader can quickly see the agenda items that were discussed. Refer to Figure 9 for an example of minutes typed in this format. Sometimes motions are underlined for easy reference.

DF 16 ITINERARY

Refer to Figure 10 for an example of a Travel Itinerary.

An itinerary is an outline showing times and activities of individuals when traveling. Usually a two-column format is used to show daily activities and their times.

A heading should be included on every page of an itinerary except for the first page. The heading should include the person's name for whom the itinerary is prepared, page number, and date.

DF 17 REPORTS

Many word processing software programs include report templates. These templates can be modified to suit the company's preferences. Most reports include a title page, table of contents page, body of the report, and back matter such as appendixes and references.

Refer to Figure 11 for an example of a report.

<u>Guidelines for Formatting General Reports</u>

1. Use a 2-inch top margin for the first page and a 1-inch top margin for the other pages of the report. Left, right, and bottom margins are usually 1 inch.

2. The title should be centered and typed in all capitals at the beginning of the report on the first page.

3. The title may be used as a header on all pages except the first page of the report and should be typed in initial capital style.

4. Double space the body of the report.

5. Triple or double space before side headings and double space after side headings. Triple spacing before side headings is the traditional report format, however, the use of computer software to produce reports has made double spacing before and after side headings the preferred style.

6. Put page numbers on all pages except the first page.

7. Single space and indent enumerated items or long quotations.

8. If portions of the text are referenced, use either footnotes or endnotes to show this.

DF 18   ENVELOPE WITH MAIL OR HANDLING NOTATIONS

See GR 7 for Address Rules and Guidelines.

Refer to Figure 12 for an example of an envelope with these notations.

A mailing notation indicates that a letter is being sent by a special mail service such as Registered, Certified, or Special Delivery.

Handling notations include such instructions as Confidential, Personal, and Hold for Arrival. Attention lines also fall into the category of handling notations.

Mailing Notations

Type the mailing notation in all-capital letters in the upper right corner of the envelope on the third line below the stamp.

Handling Notations Including Attention Notations

If the attention line is <u>not</u> typed as the first line of the address, it is treated like a handling notation.

1. Type the notation at the left, even with the return address. The notation should be typed either three lines below the return address or even with the recipient's address.

2. Type the notation in capital letters or underlined.

Refer to Figure 12 for an example of these envelope notations.

DF 19 RÉSUMÉ

In addition to the inclusion of portfolios becoming common in the job application process, electronic résumés are now mainstream. Most word processing software programs include templates for a variety of résumé styles. These template formats make it easy to quickly create a good-looking résumé. These templates, however, don't address the electronic résumé that is scanned and read by a computer.

Figures 13A, 13B, and 13C show examples of the most common traditional résumé styles, and Figure 13D shows one designed for electronic scanning. Electronic résumés sent over the Internet differ from traditional résumés in several ways. Following is a list of key points to follow when creating a résumé that will be scanned or transmitted electronically.

*   An electronic résumé is designed to produce matches found in the Keyword Summary. Since a human will not read it, it does not have to be visually appealing.

Keyword Summary: This summary consists of 20 to 30 keywords (nouns that describe job skills) and is placed at the top of the résumé directly below the job seeker's name and contact information.

Each word (noun) in the Keyword Summary should begin with a capital and end with a period. The most salable skills should be emphasized first. Job applicants should be familiar with the skills needed for the position that they are applying for and include as many of these skills that are applicable. The computer scans the résumé looking for "hits" or matches to preprogrammed skills so it is important to include words that relate to industry jargon, skills, and job postings.

Use only white paper.

Use 10-14 point font (preferred is 12 point). Use a standard font such as Helvetica. Avoid Times 10 font.

All margins should be at least a 1/2 inch.

If the résumé will be mailed and scanned rather than electronically transmitted, mail it in a flat, 9 x 12 envelope.

Omit underlining, bold, and italics

Use only one column format.

Don't justify the right margin.

Eliminate graphics, boxes, and borders.

Do not send copies of the résumé. Send only laser or high-quality printed originals.

Do not use landscape orientation.

Do not include parentheses or brackets.

RÉSUMÉ INTERNET SITES

The following are Internet sites that provide information about résumé writing, styles, and tips about the job search process.

http://jobsmart.org/tools/resume/Index.htm

http://www.jobweb.org/catapult/guenov/restips .html

http://www.iccweb.com
Go to Career Advice Articles

http://www.eresumes.com/
Go to eRésumés 101

http://www.cweb.com
Go to Career Advice at the left under Tools.

DF 20   FIGURES SHOWING LETTERS, MEMORANDUMS, MINUTES, PRESS RELEASES, AGENDAS, REPORTS, ENVELOPE FORMATS, AND RÉSUMÉS

The following pages show examples of the document formats that have been discussed.

ALISON-FULTON, INC.
189 Amberson Street
San Francisco, CA 9418
Phone: (413) 888-5550

October 7, 20—   *2 returns*

CONFIDENTIAL   *2 returns*

Mr. Thomas Johnston
879 Culver Street
San Francisco, CA 94188   *2 returns*

Dear Tom: *2 returns*

Subject: Information Concerning Job Opening   *2 returns*

The rumor you heard about Phil Anderson's leaving Alison-Fulton, Inc., is true. Phil will move to North Carolina to head the sales department of an engineering firm. There has been no official announcement regarding his departure, and his job has not been listed in any of the company's vacancy postings. I am certain that his job will not be eliminated and that within the next few weeks the position will be advertised.

Your credentials make you a strong candidate, and I think you would be granted an interview. I will keep you posted on the vacancy and will put in a good word for you when the actual selection process begins.   *2 returns*

Sincerely,   *4 returns*

Michael C. Walch   *2 returns*

rh   *2 returns*

Enclosure: Job Description of Phil's Position   *2 returns*

PS: Ed DeChant will probably be involved in hiring Phil's replacement. I'll introduce you to him at our next Rotary meeting.

Figure 1:   **Block-style letter** with subject line, confidential, enclosure, post script notations, and reference initials.

181

**Eastside Animal Hospital
88 Saint Francis Street
Newark, NJ 07105**

November 9, 20--   *2 returns*

Mr. Timothy Rodgers
One Anderson Place W.
Newark, NJ 07105   *2 returns*

Dear Mr. Rodgers:

We want to extend a special offer to our valued customers
who have more than one pet. We have implemented a multi-
pet discount for which you qualify. Mention this to the
receptionist when you bring your pets for their routine
checkup or emergency care.

We are also offering a product discount to our customers
who purchase in quantities. This discount applies to all major
lines of tick and flea control products, shampoos, and
vitamins.

As another way of saying thank you for choosing Eastside
Animal Hospital to care for your pets, we have enclosed a
coupon for a box of dog snacks.

Sincerely, *2 returns*

EASTSIDE ANIMAL HOSPITAL *4 returns*

Joseph Parsons
Administrative Assistant

lm

Enclosure

Figure 2: **Modified-block-style letter** with reference
            initials, enclosure notation, and company name
            used in closing.

182

Angel's Antiques
1001 Raynard Drive
Virginia Beach, VA 23451

January 15, 20–

Attention: East Coast Manager
ABC Auctions
3906 Beach Road
West Monroe, LA 71291   *2 returns*

Dear Sir or Madam: *2 returns*

Subject: Auction of Bettye Kriebel Estate Items   *2 returns*

This is to verify our purchase of Warehouse Lot #72, which includes items from the estate of Bettye Kriebel. Enclosed is a copy of the initial transaction.

We plan to auction this merchandise in spring and would like to have your company handle the auction. There are many valuable collectable pieces included in this merchandise, which will generate a great deal of interest. We have an agreement with Richard's Advertising to handle publicity of the auction. Please contact my assistant in Los Angeles, Ms. Martha Moorman, if you wish to inspect the merchandise prior to discussing whether or not you would be interested in handling this auction.

Sincerely,   *4 returns*

Andrea Daniels, President   *2 returns*

lc

Enclosure

c Martha Moorman

Figure 3: **Modified-block style letter with paragraph indention,** subject line, copy and enclosure notations, and attention line.

183

FLASH ELECTRONICS, INC.
6778 Lakeview Street
Detroit, MI 48220

March 13, 20–   (*4 returns*)

Mr. Steven Panrano
Richard Nameplate, Inc.
816 Commonwealth Street
Richmond, VA 23206   (*2 returns*)

DESIGN FOR FLASH NAMEPLATE   (2 returns)

Here are four drawings of nameplate artwork for three desktop
calculators, Models 112, 69, and 201.

Please quote prices for 1500 nameplates for each model; itemize
the tooling, setup, and master plate charges separately. Note that
the Flash symbol, a light bulb, is immediately below the company
name but does not touch it.

If your quotations are acceptable, the shipment should be sent by
insured mail.   (*4 returns*)

JOE SPECHT, MATERIALS SPECIALIST   (*2 returns*)

lm

Enclosures: 4

Figure 4: **Simplified letter style**. (Note: In this example, the
originator's name and job title are typed in all caps, which is
standard simplified style. It is now becoming acceptable to
type this information in initial caps instead of in all caps.)

memo:

TO: Hiram Atkins, Production Manager
              Martha Culver, Account Representative

FROM: Myron Ederly, Quality Control Analyst

DATE: June 12, 20–

SUBJECT: F36 Calculator–Defects on Light Emitting
                  Diode Display   *(2 or 3 returns)*

According to our statistical analysis, the F36 should not be inoperative or show any defects more than seven times in 1000 checks.

During the past week, the line inspectors found 84 defects in 5000 checks; all defects were related to the LED operation. In each defective calculator, one of two malfunctions existed: The numbers on the display area (1) faded away within three seconds or (2) flashed on and off.

To meet the deadline of shipment for an order in one week, the defects must be repaired immediately. All defective F36 models have been redirected to the third assembly phase for disassembly and correction. The supervisor of this phase discovered that a new employee did not follow the drawing correctly in assembling a component. I have authorized overtime in order to correct the problem, and the Accounting Department will charge this additional cost to the unit production costs for this order.

lm

C: Marlene Anderson

Figure 5: Memorandum on plain paper.

Memorandum

DATE: November 30, 20—

TO: John Russell, Vice President Marketing

FROM: Henry Bando, Marketing Manager

RE: Bicycle Accessories

CC: Store Manager: Alice Andrews

Here are the first six weeks' sales figures from our current bicycle accessories. I have included comparisons with some other nonfood departments so that you can evaluate the contribution of the Bicycle Department more accurately.

The initial results are encouraging, but where should we go from here? Should we expand promotion? Should we use the mass media (television, radio, and newspapers) to support our inside displays?

The sales figures provide only part of the data; we need to define customer reaction and manager opinion in regard to this new nonfood department. Therefore, will you please contribute this input to the program with your next report:

1. Ask 100 customers to complete the enclosed New Department Survey Form (ND 12).

2. Evaluate the contribution of this department based on
    a. the relationship to sales in other nonfood department.
    b. demographic characteristics of the population in the geographic area served by your store.

urs
Enclosures (2)

Figure 6: **Memorandum formatted using Microsoft Word template.** (Note: The copy notation is included in the heading, which is <u>not</u> standard formatting. The copy notation goes at the end of the memo between the reference initials and the enclosure notation if they are used. If the use of templates becomes mainstream, standard memo formatting may change to conform to the format used in word processing templates.)

FOR IMMEDIATE RELEASE

FROM: Heritage Inns, Inc.   **CONTACT:**
302 East Bay Street   Cynthia Northam
Edenton, NC 98321   (919) 482-4983, Ext. 28
                                Email: Nomc@aol.com
                                Fax: 919-270-2766

HERITAGE INNS TO BUILD HOTELS IN MEXICO

Edenton, NC, April 13, 2001: Ricardo Padilla, founder and board chairman of Heritage Inns, Inc., announced that the corporation will begin construction on five hotels in Mexico on October 1. These new Heritage Inns will be located in Nogales, Chihuahua, Durango, Monterrey, and Nuevo Laredo.

The stock issue is being handled by the prestigious Hyde Park Investment Company, which expects the public to clamor for entrance to its branches. Padilla announced that the corporate policy, which he has espoused from the beginning of his career, will be maintained in the Mexican operation. The policy is expected to provide an economic "shot in the arm" to many communities throughout the country.

###

Figure 7: Press Release.

Many word processing software programs have templates that format press releases. This example shows a typical format to use when not using a template.

187

```
┌─────────────────────────────────────────────────┐
│                                                 │
│                   AGENDA                        │
│                                                 │
│                                                 │
│   FACULTY COUNCIL MEETING                       │
│   4 p.m., May 1, 20–                            │
│   Room 150 Keller Building                      │
│                                                 │
│   1. Approval of Minutes                        │
│                                                 │
│   2. Election to Committee Vacancies:           │
│                                                 │
│           Scholarship Committee                 │
│           Instructional Development committee   │
│                                                 │
│   3. Announcement of Faculty Fellowship Awards  │
│                                                 │
│   4. Budget Report                              │
│                                                 │
│       Items                       Disposition   │
│                                                 │
│       Conference Reports           _____    │
│       Mileage Increases            _____    │
│       Capital Equipment Requests   _____    │
│       Building Improvement Request _____    │
│                                                 │
│   5. Announcements                              │
│                                                 │
│   Note:  Council members are asked to bring a copy of the │
│   Faculty Handbook and the attached budget report to the  │
│   meeting.                                      │
│                                                 │
│   Attachment                                    │
│                                                 │
└─────────────────────────────────────────────────┘
```

Figure 8: Agenda.

Some word processing software programs have templates that automatically format agendas.

MINUTES OF THE CITIZEN'S NATIONAL BANK
EXECUTIVE BOARD MEETING
SEPTEMBER 19, 20—
MARRIOTT INN SOUTH, ORLANDO, FLORIDA

CALL TO ORDER
ROLL CALL

President John Sanders called the meeting to order at 6 p.m. Members present were Sandra Fain, Melvin Thompson, Wanda Jackson, Dorothy Showalter, and John Chojnacki. Members absent were Liz Tyler, and Stan Fiitz.

APPROVAL OF
MINUTES

Minutes of the last meeting were approved as submitted.

EXECUTIVE
SESSION

President Sanders called the Board into executive session. Agenda Item 1 concerning new federal policy regulations on HUD loans was reviewed. Discussion followed concerning how these new federal regulations will change current documentation tracking practices and the effect

(underline motions and/or type the words "MOTION", "RESOLVED", and "PASSED" in all capitals.)

these new regulations will have on loans. <u>It was moved by Dorothy Showalter and seconded by Wanda Jackson that these new policy changes be studied in order to determine how to best implement them. Motion carried.</u>

TREASURER'S
REPORT

After explanations of several budget items, the treasurer's report was accepted as presented.

AGENDA ITEMS

Agenda Item 4 (Bylaw Revisions) was tabled to the next meeting.

NEW BUSINESS

Discussion was held about sponsoring scholarships.

ADJOURNMENT

The meeting was adjourned at 9:30 p.m.

Respectfully submitted,

Dorothy Showalter, Secretary

Figure 9: Minutes.

TRAVEL ITINERARY
DR. PAUL MULHOLLAND

April 1-10, 20—
Boston–New York–Pittsburgh

TUESDAY, APRIL 1

8 a.m.	Depart Boston on United Airlines Flight AA/147 to Pittsburgh.
9:30 a.m.	Arrive Pittsburgh. Take shuttle to Hilton East Hotel. Confirmation #28709.
Noon-2 p.m.	Lunch with Dr. Anna Hughes, Dr. Laura Salerno, and Dr. Anthony Weissman, associate staff members from Princeton Medical Clinic. Obtain input from their view concerning what they see as priority in terms of equipment and facility needs in upgrading Eastside's outpatient clinic.

WEDNESDAY, APRIL 2

9 a.m.-10:30 a.m.	Tour the new Central Medical Center. Contrast this new center with the current operating conditions of Eastside's outpatient clinic's treatment capabilities and facilities. Dr. Tom Ruben will be your guide.
1 p.m.	Depart Pittsburgh for a direct flight to New York (United Airlines Flight DS/126).
2:30 p.m.	Arrive in New York. Harry Poter will meet plane and take you to the Embassy Hotel. Confirmation #873AB.

Figure 10: Travel Itinerary.

190

(Type title 2 inches from top of paper–2 inch top margin)

VIDEOCONFERENCING ETIQUETTE
(3 returns after title)

Video conferencing is a viable and accessible meeting option today. The high cost of travel, coupled with fast-paced global business, has made video conferencing popular. Below are some hints to keep in mind when participating in a video-conference.

<u>Room Setup</u>

Room and seating arrangements are always important elements in the success of a videoconference. A standard boardroom setting (attendees seated around a conference table) is one option. Another option is a panel setup where participants seated at a table face the camera.

Another possibility is a "living room" arrangement with a few armchairs positioned around a coffee table. This setup may not be appropriate for some business meetings.

<u>Video Manners</u>

Video magnifies makeup, gestures, and speech patterns. Even clothes should be considered when appearing in a videoconference. The following are tips that will assist in preparing for a successful videoconference.

Figure 11: Report (page one).

(one inch top margin)

- Choose conservative clothing. Bright tones and patterns are more intense on screen and may not show true colors: greens can turn to a sickly blue and reds can change into a garish orange. Stick with neutral suits in navy or gray with a solid pale-colored silk blouse. Dangling jewelry should not be worn.

- Dress in appropriate business attire. Even if usual office wear is casual, it is better to dress up.

- Face the camera. Know where the video camera is and make certain that participants address the correct camera. Also, squirming, shifting, and fast movements will cause the televised image to be blurred.

- Watch expressions and nervous habits. Everything is exaggerated on camera. The mannerisms that go unnoticed in regular meetings are magnified on camera. Gestures such as chewing on a pencil or the stem of eyeglasses, biting nails, or twirling strands of hair do not go unnoticed on camera.

It is also a good idea to practice if a formal presentation is to be done. This will prevent the "talking head" scenario and allow participants to present their best image. Practicing good body language and good speech and delivery will make the video conference much more professional.

Figure 11: Report (page 2).

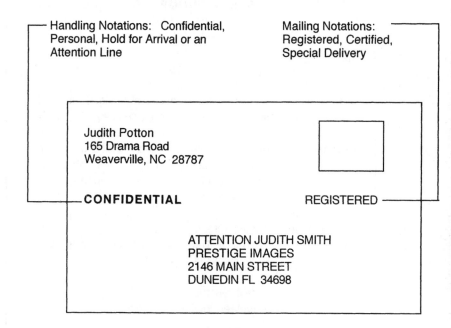

Figure 12: Envelope

SUSAN THOMPSON
870 Breezeway Dr.
Winfield, KS 67156
(314) 221-4565
Email: ThompsonS@aol.com

Objective	An administrative assistant position with professional growth opportunities.
Summary	Recent graduate with secretarial and desktop publishing expertise. Team player with excellent interpersonal, communication, organizational, and leadership skills.
Professional Experience	August 1999 to Present Secretary, <u>Temporary Staffing, Winfield, KS</u> Part-time while in school June 1998-1999 Volunteer, <u>YMCA, Winefield, KS</u>
Education	June 2000–Associate of Science Degree <u>Apex Community College</u> June 1998–Diploma <u>Dixie Jones High School</u> Winefield, KS

Special Skills	Mous certified
	Keyboarding 65 wpm
	Software: Microsoft Office 2000
	            PageMaker 6.5 Plus
	            QuarkXPress 4.1
	Business Accounting
	Transcription

References	Available upon request

Figure 13A: Chronological Résumé.

194

SUSAN THOMPSON

870 Breezeway Dr.   Phone: (314) 221-4565
Winfield, KS 67156   Email: ThompsonS@aol.com

Objective   An administrative assistant position with
                       professional growth opportunities.

Summary   Recent graduate with secretarial and desktop
                       publishing expertise. Team player with
                       excellent interpersonal communication,
                       organizational and leadership skills.

Special   Mous certified
Skills   Keyboarding 65 wpm
                       Software: Microsoft Office 2000
                                   PageMaker 6.5 Plus
                                   QuarkXPress 4.1
                       Business Accounting
                       Transcription

Professional   August 1999 to Present
Experience   Secretary, Temporary Staffing, Winfield. KS
                       Part-time while in school

                       June 1998-1999
                       Volunteer, YMCA, Winefield, KS

Education   June 2000–Associate of Science Degree
                       Apex Community College
                       Winefield, KS

                       June 1998–Diploma
                       Dixie Jones High School
                       Winefield, KS

References   Available upon request

Figure 13B: Functional Résumé.

195

SUSAN THOMPSON
870 Breezeway Dr.   Winfield, KS 67156
Phone: (314) 221-4565   Email: ThompsonS@aol.com

SUMMARY

Recent graduate with secretarial and desktop publishing expertise. Academic background includes handling multiple projects and meeting deadlines, planning events, producing presentations, designing brochures, and writing newsletters. Team player with excellent interpersonal, communication, organizational, and leadership skills.

SPECIAL SKILLS

- Mous certified
- Event and Volunteer Coordination
- Promotional Materials
- Customer Relations
- Microsoft Office 2000, PageMaker 6.5 Plus, QuarkXPress 4.1

HIGHLIGHTS

- Served in a leadership role in Phi Beta Lambda, a national business student organization
- Published author of a Business Tips column for college newspaper
- Provided administrative support for local YMCA branch
- Designed promotional materials resulting in increased volunteer activities

PROFESSIONAL EXPERIENCE, FULL AND PART-TIME

Secretary, Temporary Staffing, Winfield, KS (2000 to Present)
Provided secretarial support to local businesses, such as Lockheed Martin, Grandview Pines Hotel, West Shores Marketing, and TYME.

Volunteer, Admin. Support, YMCA, Winefield, KS (2000 to Present)
Part-time while in school (weekends)
Receptionist and volunteer coordinator. Developed a volunteer marketing campaign that included print and multimedia advertising. Developed PowerPoint presentation with Visual Thunder software and presented this multimedia presentation to local businesses.

Figure 13C: Combination/Skills Résumé Page 1

EDUCATION
Associate of Science Degree, Major: Administrative Assistant
Apex Community College, Winefield, KS
Graduated with Honors, June 2001

High School Diploma
Dixie Jones High School, Winefield, KS
June 1999

PROFESSIONAL AFFILIATIONS
President, PBL (post secondary business student organization)
Public Relations Committee Chair, YMCA Volunteer Campaign Project

AWARDS AND RECOGNITION
Academic scholarship awarded by Orange County Public Schools
First place district competition in Ms. Future Business Leader event
YMCA volunteer campaign won first place from 17 entries

REFERENCES

Dr. Lawerence Lychako   Ms. Judy Mathis-Lambert, Director
Apex Community College   East Orange YMCA
P.O. Box 2897   P.O. Box 398A
Winefield, KS 70165   Winefield, KS 72914
Phone: (707-289-6120)   Phone: (707-593-4961)

                    Ms. Paula Viejo, Production Coordinator
                    Planet Digital
                    3500 Technology Row
                    Winefield, KS 70165
                    Phone: (707-264-7731)

PORTFOLIO AVAILABLE UPON REQUEST

Figure 13C: Combination/Skills Résumé Page 2

Trend is to use "References Available Upon Request" although
it is still acceptable to list references on résumé.

SUSAN THOMPSON
870 Breezeway Dr.
Winfield, KS 67156
(314) 221-4565
Email: ThompsonS@aol.com

Keywords: Administrative Assistant. Executive Secretary. Office Support. Mous certification. Computer Skills. Word. Excel. Power-Point. Access. PageMaker. QuarkXPress. Desktop Publishing. Excellent communication, phone skills. Strong organizational skills. Detail oriented. Customer relations. Team player. Strong work ethic.

Goal: An administrative assistant position with professional growth opportunities.

Education:
Associate of Science Degree
Major: Administrative Assistant
Apex Community College, Winefield, KS
Graduated with Honors, June 2001

High School Diploma
Dixie Jones High School, Winefield, KS
June 1999

Experience:
Secretary
Temporary Staffing, Winfield, KS, 2000 to Present
Provided secretarial support to local businesses such as Lockheed Martin, Grandview Pines Hotel, West Shores Marketing, and TYME.

Volunteer, Administrative Support
YMCA, Winefield, KS, 2000 to Present
Part-time while in school (weekends)
Receptionist and volunteer coordinator. Developed a volunteer marketing campaign that included print and multimedia advertising. Developed PowerPoint presentation with Visual Thunder software and presented this multimedia presentation to local businesses.

Figure 13D: Keyword (Electronic) Résumé, Page 1.

Special Skills

Event and Volunteer Coordination
Promotional Materials
Customer Relations
Computer Literate: Microsoft Office 2002, PageMaker 6.5 Plus,
QuarkXPress 4.1

Experience Highlights

Served in a leadership role in Phi Beta Lambda, a national business
student organization
Published author of a Business Tips column for college newspaper
Provided administrative support for local YMCA branch
Designed promotional materials resulting in increased volunteer
activities

Professional Affiliations

President, Phi Beta Lambda
Public Relations Committee Chair, YMCA Volunteer Campaign Project

Awards and Recognition

Academic scholarship awarded by Orange County Public School
First place district competition in Ms. Future Business Leader event
YMCA volunteer campaign won first place from 17 entries

References

Available upon request.

Portfolio Available Upon Request

Figure 13D: Keyword (Electronic) Résumé, Page 2.

FILING
PROCEDURES

FP 1 FILING PROCEDURES AND SUPPLIES

FP1.1 STEPS IN THE FILING PROCESS

The filing process may begin with processing incoming mail. Before correspondence can be filed, it must be coded so that it can be sorted according to alphabetic, numeric, geographic, or subject filing rules. Generally before mail is filed, it has to be released or approved by someone for filing so that correspondence requiring action is not filed before proper response has been taken.

There are five steps in the filing process:

1. **Inspecting**: All incoming correspondence should be checked to be sure that it has been released for filing. Usually the person with authority to release the correspondence for filing writes his or her initials in the left corner of the document.

2. **Indexing**: Indexing is the process of determining the name (caption) under which the correspondence will be filed. Generally documents are filed by:

   - The name of the person who wrote the letter.
   - The name of the person to whom the letter is addressed.
   - The name of the company in correspondence received.
   - A subject discussed in the letter.
   - A geographic location.

3. **Coding**: Coding is the process of writing, underlining, or highlighting the name (caption) under which the correspondence was indexed and will be filed. Sometimes it may be necessary to *cross reference* a document when there is more than one logical place it can be filed. See FP 6 for information about cross referencing.

4. **Sorting**: Sorting is the process of arranging the documents according to their captions for filing. There are commercial aides available to help sort documents quickly into alphabetic, numeric, or subject categories.

5. Storing: Storing is the process of filing the documents by putting them into the proper folders in file cabinets. Below are guides to follow when filing correspondence within folders:

- Arrange correspondence alphabetically by name or subject.
- If there is more than one piece of correspondence for the same name or subject, the most recent item according to date should be filed in front.

FP 1.2 FILING SUPPLIES

Guides are sturdy dividers with tabs that have captions. Guides separate groups of file folders in a file drawer. There are two types of guides: *primary* and *special*. Primary guides are used as the main dividers in the file drawer. They could be the letters of the alphabet in an alphabetical filing system or names of categories in a subject filing system. Special guides are used to identify subdivisions behind the primary guides. Examples of primary and special guides in an alphabetical filing system could be B (Primary) Be (Special), Bi (Special). Examples of primary and special guides in a subject filing system could be Employment (Primary) Active Applications (Special), Inactive Applications (Special), Employment Forms (Special).

File Folders are used to organize documents filed behind the appropriate guides. Folders, like guides, have tabs on them and contain documents sorted by company name, individual name, subject, number, or geographic location. General folders are folders used to file documents for which there are no special folders. For instance, behind the primary guide "S" there are individual folders for Southwest Academy, Southern Baptist College, and Southern Middelton Academy. A document coded South Bay University needs to be filed. Since there is no special (individual) folder for South Bay University, it would be filed in the "S" general folder.

FP 2 ALPHABETIC FILING

FP 2.1 INDEXING UNITS

Rules have been established for filing documents to standardize principles. The Association of Records Managers and Administrators (ARMA) has defined procedures to use in breaking down the name that a document is to be filed into parts called indexing units.

Below are the ARMA indexing unit rules that have become standard in business. Noting discrepancies between these rules and those in some textbooks and reference guides (especially the rule concerning the treatment of articles, prepositions, and conjunctions), the author contacted ARMA to be sure that the rules in this Office Guide are official ARMA rules that are approved by the American National Standards Institute.

FP 2.2 NOTHING COMES BEFORE SOMETHING

A letter by itself comes before a word or name that begins with that letter. Similarly, one word comes before two words, and two words come before three words, etc.

Example: Arranged in order according to rule.

Name	Unit 1	Unit 2	Unit 3
A	A		
Anderson	Anderson		
Video Support	Video	Support	
Video Support Time	Video	Support	Time
Videos West	Videos	West	

FP 2.3 NAMES WITH PUNCTUATION

> Ignore all punctuation including hyphens, diagonals, apostrophes, commas, and periods when alphabetizing.

Example: Arranged in order according to rule.

Name	Unit 1	Unit 2
Import/Export Art	ImportExport	Art
In-The-Red Solutions	InTheRed	Solutions
O'Leary Imports	OLeary	Imports
O'Leary's Deli	Olearys	Deli
South Photos	South	Photos
South-Western Photos	Southwestern	Photos
Teachers' Gifts	Teachers	Gifts
Teacher's Pet	Teachers	Pet

FP 2.4 ARTICLES/MINOR WORDS

> Prepositions (on, at, to, by, for, in, of), conjunctions (and, or), and articles (a, an, the) are used as indexing units. If *a, an,* or *the* is the *first* word in a name, it becomes the *last* indexing unit.

Example: Arranged in order according to rule.

Name	Unit 1	Unit 2	Unit 3	Unit 4
The Big Red Boat	Big	Red	Boat	The
The Class Matters	Class	Matters	The	
The Classic Rock Station	Classic	Rock	Station	The
Classroom T's and Z's	Classroom	Ts	and	Zs
In The Red House	In	The	Red	House
An Inspiration	Inspiration	An		
A Matter of Class	Matter	of	Class	A
A Perfect Picture	Perfect	Picture	A	

FP 2.5 PERSONAL NAMES (GENERAL)

> The order for indexing units in personal names is: last name, first name or initial, middle name or initial.

Example: Arranged in order according to rule.

Name	Unit 1	Unit 2	Unit 3
A. David Mallinson	Mallinson	A	David
David Mallinson	Mallinson	David	
R. Dan Mallinson	Mallinson	R	Dan
B. C. Roger	Roger	B	C
Bart C. Roger	Roger	Bart	C

FP 2.6 PERSONAL NAMES USED IN BUSINESSES AND ORGANIZATIONS

> Index personal names used in business and in organizations in the *same* order as written.

Example: Arranged in order according to rule.

Name	Unit 1	Unit 2	Unit 3	Unit 4
Baki-Abet AD Agency	BakiAbet	AD	Agency	
J. Tally Video	J	Tally	Video	
Ms. Smith's Cookies	Ms.	Smiths	Cookies	
Nancy's Tye-Dye, Inc.	Nancys	TyeDye	Inc.	
Robert Jones Auto Shop	Robert	Jones	Auto	Shop
Wanda Courdy Inn	Wanda	Courdy	Inn	

FP 2.7 PREFIXES IN NAMES AND BUSINESSES

> Prefixes such as *d', D', Da, de, De, Del, La, Las, Los, Mac, Mc, Saint, San, Van der,* and *Von* are considered as one indexing unit, even if spaces are used with the prefix. Do not spell out abbreviations such as St.

Example: Arranged in order according to rule.

Name	Unit 1	Unit 2	Unit 3
Ryan De Perro	DePerro	Ryan	
Marie D'Errico	Derrico	Marie	
Rosa M. De La Cruz	DeLaCruz	Rosa	M.
Luz C. De Voto	DeVoto	Luz	C
G. McPerson Motors	G	McPerson	Motors
Las Vegas Motel	LasVegas	Motel	
Ronald T. Mac Allister	MacAllister	Ronald	T
Susan MacAllister	MacAllister	Susan	
Patrick M'Cauley	MCauley	Patrick	
Mary St. Claire Hosp.	Mary	St.Claire	Hosp.
Tan Ming Ho	MingHo	Tan	
Anthony Saint Claire	SaintClaire	Anthony	
Santa Fe College	SantaFe	College	
Annette St. Clair	StClair	Annette	

FP 2.8 HYPHENATED NAMES

> Hyphenated names are treated as one unit.

Example: Arranged in order according to rule.

Name	Unit 1	Unit 2	Unit 3
J. R. Anders-Smith	Anders-Smith	J.	R.
Jean-Louis Macon	Macon	Jean Louis	
Nancy O'Leary-Suz	OLearySuz	Nancy	
Jean-Pierre Riviere	Riviere	Jean-Pierre	
R. T. Ruiz-Walters	RuizWalters	R	T
Wong Yat-ming	Yatming	Wong	

FP 2.9　PERSONAL NAMES WITH TITLES

Titles such as *Miss, Mr., Ms., Dr., Prof., Rev., Queen, Princess, Prince,* and *Mayor* are indexed *last* when a first and last name are included. When no last name is given, the title is used as the *first* indexing unit. Do not spell out abbreviated titles.

Example:　Arranged in order according to rule.

Name	Unit 1	Unit 2	Unit 3	Unit 4
Dr. Tom J. Albers	Albers	Tom	J.	Dr.
Dr. Suess	Dr.	Suess		
Senator Toni Fox	Fox	Toni	Senator	
Major T. Leslie	Leslie	T.	Major	
Mayor Paul	Mayor	Paul		
Princess Diane	Princess	Diane		
Rabbi Sol	Rabbi	Sol		
Mr. Jon Royal	Royal	Jon	Mr.	
Ms. Jon Royal	Royal	Jon	Ms.	
Saint Eliza	Saint	Eliza		

FP 2.10　ABBREVIATIONS

Abbreviated names are indexed as written regardless of spacing.

Example:　Arranged in order according to rule.

Name	Unit 1	Unit 2	Unit 3
AAA	AAA		
Capt. Ed's Seafood	Capt.	Eds	Seafood
Ft. Brag Video	Ft.	Brag	Video
NAACP	NAACP		
Wm. Tuck	Tuck	Wm.	

FP 2.11   SENIORITY AND ACADEMIC TERMS

> Seniority terms such as *Jr., Sr., 2d, 3d, IV,* and academic terms such as *M.D., Ph.D.,* and *CPA* are indexed after the first name.

> Numeric units come *before* alphabetic units, and arabic numerals come before roman numerals. See rule FP 2.13.

Example: Arranged in order according to rule.

Name	Unit 1	Unit 2	Unit 3	Unit 4
Prof. Alice Andrews, Ph.D.	Andrews	Alice	Ph.D.	Prof.
T. Green, IV	Green	T	IV	
Thomas Green, Sr.	Green	Thomas	Sr.	
Dr. Jim Norton, 2nd	Norton	Jim	2nd	Dr.
Sally Norton, M.D.	Norton	Sally	MD	
Sam Norton, 2d	Norton	Sam	2d	
Sam Norton, IV	Norton	Sam	IV	
Dr. Sam Norton, IV	Norton	Sam	IV	Dr.
Sam Norton, M.D.	Norton	Sam	MD	

FP 2.12   SYMBOLS USED IN NAMES

> Symbols are treated as one unit if there is no space between the number and symbol. Symbols are spelled out. Examples: & (and), ¢ (cent or cents), $ (dollar or dollars), # (number or pounds) % (percent), + (plus). When $ comes before a number, the number comes before the word *dollar* or *dollars.* Example: $10 Stop Gap (10dollar, Stop Gap). Numbers are indexed before alphabetic units.

Example: Arranged in order according to rule.

Name	Unit 1	Unit 2	Unit 3	Unit 4
The $7 Store	7dollar	Store	The	
55% Outlet	55percent	Outlet		
Corner 5 & 10	Corner	5	and	10
Macy's 5&10	Macys	5And10		
A #1 Grocery	Number1	Grocery	A	

FP 2.13 NAMES WITH NUMERALS

Numbers come before alphabetic units, and Arabic numerals (1, 2, 3) come before roman numerals. Do not include ordinals. Example: 1st is indexed as 1.

If a unit has a number and a word joined by punctuation, it is treated as one unit.

Numbers are indexed in numeric order. If a unit contains two numbers joined by punctuation, only use the number *before* the punctuation. Example: 20/20 News is indexed as 20 news.

Example: Arranged in order according to rule.

Name	Unit 1	Unit 2	Unit 3
1 Hour Photo	1	Hour	Photo
1A Answering	1A	Answering	
4 Season Event	4	Season	Event
The 5 Ave.	5	Ave	The
21st Century Video	21	Century	Video
210 Hills Lounge	210	Hills	Lounge
250-300 Sales Club	250	Sales	Club
IV Brothers Deli	IV	Brothers	Deli
Ninth Street Fashion	Ninth	Street	Fashion
Three Brothers Deli	Three	Brothers	Deli
Two East Cafe	Two	East	Cafe

FP 2.14 FEDERAL GOVERNMENT NAMES

Use United States Government as the first three indexing units for any federal government agency even though these words are not included in the name.

The next unit after United States Government is the *name* of the department, office, or bureau.

The units following the name of the department, office, or bureau are the words: department, office, or bureau if these were included in the name.

Example: Arranged in order according to rule. First three indexing units (United States Government) are not shown.

Name	Unit 4	Unit 5	Unit 6	Unit 7
Department of Agriculture	Agri-culture	Depart-ment	Of	
Department of Commerce	Com-merce	Depart-ment	Of	
Office of Consumer Affairs	Con-sumer	Affairs	Office	Of
Federal Bureau of Investigation	Federal	Bureau	Of	Investiga-tion
Bureau of Indian Affairs	Indian	Affairs	Bureau	Of
National Park Service	National	Park	Service	
Bureau of Prisons	Prisons	Bureau	Of	
Social Security Administration	Social	Security	Admin-istration	

FP 2.15   STATE AND LOCAL GOVERNMENT NAMES

> The first indexing unit should be the name of the state, city, town, or county.

> If the word *state, county, city,* or *town* is used in the name, it becomes the next indexing unit, followed by the <u>name</u> of the department, bureau, or office.

> The units following the name of the department, office, or bureau are the words: department, office, or bureau, if these were included in the name.

Example: Arranged in order according to rule.

Name	Unit 1	Unit 2	Unit 3	Unit 4
Fla. State Dept. of Ed.	Fla.	State	Ed.	Dept.
Illinois Div. of Labor	Illinois	Labor	Division	Of
New York City Transportation	New	York	City	Trans-portation
Orange Co. Parks and Recreation	Orange	Co.	Parks	and
Registry of Deeds, Sumter County	Sumter	County	Deeds	Registry

FP 3   NUMERIC FILING

FP 3.1   NUMERIC FILING PROCEDURES

Generally the first step in numeric filing is to assign a number to a category, individual, or topic. For instance, if a company did business with several clients, a number could be assigned to each client. Documents would be coded with the number assigned to the client and filed numerically. An alphabetic index is used to quickly see what numbers have been assigned to an individual, company, or category. A log called an accession log is used to keep track of the numbers assigned so that numbers are not duplicated. Because a numeric filing system is an indirect system, it helps maintain security.

FP 3.2   CONSECUTIVE NUMERIC ORDER

Large numbers are frequently divided into groups of three digits. In the consecutive filing method, numbers are filed first by the first group of digits, and then by the second group of digits, and finally by the last group of digits.

Example: Arranged in order according to rule.

Number	Unit 1	Unit 2	Unit 3
178987126	178	987	126
458986437	458	986	437

FP 3.3   MIDDLE-DIGIT ORDER

Numbers are filed numerically by the middle group of digits, and then by the first group of digits, and finally by the last group of digits.

Example: Arranged in order according to rule.

Number	Unit 1	Unit 2	Unit 3
458986437	986	458	437
178987126	987	178	126

FP 3.4   TERMINAL-DIGIT ORDER

Numbers are filed numerically by the <u>last</u> group of digits then by the second group of digits, and finally by the first group of digits.

Example: Arranged in order according to rule.

Number	Unit 1	Unit 2	Unit 3
178987126	126	987	178
458986437	437	986	458

FP 4   GEOGRAPHIC FILING

FP 4.1   DICTIONARY ARRANGEMENT

In the dictionary arrangement of geographic filing, geographic names are filed alphabetically by geographic location.

Example: Arranged in order according to rule.

Name	Guide	Unit 1	Unit 2
Alaska	A	Alaska	
Colorado	C	Colorado	
Florida	F	Florida	

FP 4.2   ENCYCLOPEDIA ARRANGEMENT

In the encyclopedia arrangement of geographic filing, the filing order begins with the largest geographic territory to the smallest. For example: first the country; second the state or province; and last individual folders containing information about a specific client, agency, etc. Street names are used only when the other units are identical.

Example: Arranged in order according to rule.

Address	Unit 1	Unit 2	Unit 3	Unit 4
Mallison Deli 86 Earth Drive Chicago, IL 36290	IL	Chicago	Mallison	Deli
Rainbow Inn 23 Eastwind Circle Tampa, FL 37497	FL	Tampa	Rainbow	Inn

FP 5   SUBJECT FILING

FP 5.1   DICTIONARY ARRANGEMENT

Files are filed alphabetically by folder names behind alphabetic guides.

Example: Arranged in order according to rule.

Folder Name	Guide	Unit 1	Unit 3
Dell	D	Dell	
WordPerfect	W	WordPerfect	
HP DeskJet	H	HP DeskJet	

FP 5.2   ENCYCLOPEDIA ARRANGEMENT

Files are filed alphabetically first by a main category
and then by one or more categories in a subgroup.

Example: Arranged in order according to rule.

Folder Name	Guide 1	Guide 2	Unit 3
Dell	H	Hardware	Dell
WordPerfect	S	Software	WordPerfect
HP DeskJet	P	Printers	HP DeskJet

FP 6   CROSS-REFERENCING

The yellow pages of the telephone book are filled with
examples of cross-references. For instance, information
about cars could be found under automobiles, transportation, names of specific cars, or motor vehicles. It would be
impractical to file the information in all these categories, so
cross-referencing is used to direct individuals to the
caption under which the information can be found.

FP 6.1 PERSONAL NAMES

When it is difficult to determine an individual's first or
last name, it is appropriate to use cross-referencing.

Example:

Name: Tom Daniel
Filed Under: Daniel, Tom
Cross Reference: Tom Daniel. See Daniel, Tom

Name: Yew Wong
Filed Under: Wong, Yew
Cross Reference: Yew, Wong. See Wong, Yew

FP 6.2 ABBREVIATIONS

> When an acronym or abbreviation is commonly used to refer to an organization, it is appropriate to cross-reference the organization's name with the acronym or abbreviation.

Example:

> Internal Revenue Service
> See IRS

FP 6.3 BUSINESS NAMES

> When a business includes several names, cross-referencing helps find files when only one name is remembered.

Example of one cross -reference:

> Anderson, Smith, Gleason
>
> See: Smith, Anderson, Gleason

INDEX

219

241

242

Scholarship
recipients

individual
Regret

etc.   denot

and so on
So on